CHILDREN
OF THE
FUTURE

WILHELM REICH

CHILDREN
OF THE
FUTURE

On the Prevention of
Sexual Pathology

With translations by Derek and Inge Jordan
and Beverly Placzek

Edited by Mary Higgins and Chester M. Raphael, M.D.

Preface by William Steig

FARRAR STRAUS GIROUX
New York

Library of Congress Cataloging in Publication Data

Reich, Wilhelm, 1897–1957.
    Children of the future.
    1. Sex (Psychology). 2. Child psychology.
3. Adolescent psychology. 4. Sexual deviation.
I. Higgins, Mary. II. Raphael, Chester M. III. Title.
BF723.S4R4413 1983   616.85'8305   83–8899

Love, work and knowledge are the wellsprings of our life. They should also govern it.

WILHELM REICH

Contents

Preface by William Steig

How do babies, those beautiful, guileless creatures of joy, develop into us—insecure, self-involved people, incapable of living together in harmony, with ambitions to become unusually wealthy, or terribly clever, or enviably beautiful, or world-famous for some reason or other, eventually wanting to find God (who is presumably in hiding somewhere) and hoping our children will not turn out like us?

Angels at birth, we become lost souls. And so it has been for ever so long, as we learn from reading the ancients. How does this happen? Why do we humans, in many ways the most intelligent of all animals, fail to realize what every dog, or whale, or mouse spontaneously knows—that he is part of nature and must cooperate with it, obey its laws? Why are we estranged from life? What is wrong with us, with our way of rearing our children?

Reich asked such questions all the time. He was one of those extraordinary men who are able to step outside their culture and examine it with innocent eyes.

This book contains a part of Reich's enormous work on human pathology. It consists of studies, made between 1926 and 1952, of the damage we do to our children by thwarting their natural impulses, some of which are sexual.

These studies are of more than passing interest. In a world where nations are preparing to obliterate one another and the planet itself in order to assert, quite emphatically, their various ideological points of view, it is proper for us to ardently consider everything that helps us understand how we got into this terrifying position.

January 1983

Children of the future age,
Reading this indignant page,
Know that in a former time,
Love, sweet love, was thought a crime.

WILLIAM BLAKE

I have throughout all of my lifetime loved infants and children and adolescents, and I also was always loved and understood by them. Infants used to smile at me because I had deep contact with them, and children of two or three very often used to become thoughtful and serious when they looked at me. This was one of the great happy privileges of my life, and I want to express in some manner my thanks for that love bestowed upon me by my little friends. May fate and the great ocean of living energy, from whence they came and into which they must return sooner or later, bless them with happiness and contentment and freedom during their lifetime. I hope to have contributed my good share to their future happiness.

WILHELM REICH,
from his will

CHILDREN
OF THE
FUTURE

The Source of
the Human "No"

When a child is born, it comes out of a warm uterus, 37
degrees centigrade, into about 18 or 20 degrees centigrade.
That's bad enough. The shock of birth . . . bad enough. But
it could survive that if the following didn't happen: As it
comes out, it is picked up by the legs and slapped on the
buttocks. The first greeting is a slap. The next greeting:
Take it away from the mother. Right? Take it away from
the mother. I want you to listen here. It will sound incred-
ible in a hundred years. Take it away from the mother. The
mother must not touch or see the baby. The baby has no
body contact after having had nine months of body contact at a very high temperature—what we call the "orgonotic body energy contact," the field action between them,
the warmth and the heat. Then, the Jews introduced something about six or seven thousand years ago. And that is
circumcision. I don't know why they introduced it. It's still
a riddle. Take that poor penis. Take a knife—right? And
start cutting. And everybody says, "It doesn't hurt." Everybody says, "No, it doesn't hurt." Get it? That's an excuse,
of course, a subterfuge. They say that the sheaths of the
nerve are not yet developed. Therefore, the sensation in
the nerves is not yet developed. Therefore, the child doesn't
feel a thing. Now, that's murder! Circumcision is one of the
worst treatments of children. And what happens to them?
You just look at them. They can't talk to you. They just cry.

3

What they do is shrink. They contract, get away into the inside, away from that ugly world. I express it very crudely, but you understand what I mean. Now, that's the greeting: Taking it away from the mother. Mother mustn't see it. Twenty-four or forty-eight hours, eat nothing. Right? Penis cut. And then comes the worst: This poor child, poor infant, tries always to stretch out and to find some warmth, something to hold on to. It goes to the mother, puts its lips to the mother's nipple. And what happens? The nipple is cold, or doesn't erect, or the milk doesn't come, or the milk is bad. And that is quite general. That is not one case in a thousand. That is general. That's average. So what does that infant do? How does it respond to that? How does it have to respond to that bioenergetically? It can't come to you and tell you, "Oh, listen, I'm suffering so much, so much." It doesn't say "no" in words, you understand, but that is the emotional situation. And we orgonomists know it. We get it out of our patients. We get it out of their emotional structure, out of their behavior, not out of their words. Words can't express it. Here, in the very beginning, the spite develops. Here, the "no" develops, the big "NO" of humanity. And then you ask why the world is in a mess.

Children of the Future*

The fate of the human race will be shaped by the character structures of the Children of the Future. In their hands and hearts the great decisions will lie. They will have to clean up the mess of this twentieth century. This concerns us who are living today in the middle of this great mess.

During the past century, our parents and grandparents have repeatedly tried to penetrate the wall of social evil with all kinds of social theories, political programs, reforms, resolutions, and revolutions. They have failed miserably every time; not one attempt at an improvement of the human lot has succeeded. More than that, or rather, worse than that, the misery became deeper and the entanglement worse with every new attempt. The present generation, i.e., those who are in their maturity today, the thirty- to sixty-year-olds, have inherited the confusion and tried hard but in vain to get out of it. Some have been able to raise their heads above the chaos, others have been dragged into the whirlpool, never to emerge again. In other words, *we have failed miserably as builders of a new orientation in life.* We were too much burdened with our own past entanglements. We have carried chains on our legs while we tried desperately to jump into freedom. We fell, and as a generation, we shall never make it.

* Report on the Orgonomic Infant Research Center, given by Wilhelm Reich at the Second International Orgonomic Conference, August 25, 1950.

Is there, then, no hope at all? There *is* hope, much hope, if only we muster the courage and the decency to realize our miserable failure. Then, and only then, shall we be able to see where and how we can pitch in and *help*.

We can help if we realize fully the tremendous hope entailed in an entirely new, hitherto unheard-of kind of social development which has entered the scene: *The international interest in the child.* This development began in 1946 in the United States, shortly after the end of World War II.

The first requirement for grasping the given opportunities in this new development is the realization of our proper function: We are no more than transmission belts from an evil past to an eventually better future. We shall not be the ones to build this future. We have no right to tell our children how to build their future, since we have proved unfit to build our own present. What we can do, however, is to tell our children exactly where and how we failed. And we can do everything possible to remove the obstacles which are in their way to building a new, better world for themselves.

We cannot possibly preach "cultural adaptation" for our children when this very same culture has been disintegrating under our feet for more than thirty-five years. Should our children adapt to this age of war, mass killing, tyranny, and moral deterioration?

We cannot possibly hope to build independent human characters if education is in the hands of politicians. We cannot, and dare not, give away our children in such a shabby manner.

We cannot tell our children what kind of world they will or should build. But we *can* equip them with the kind of character structure and biological vigor which will enable them to make *their own* decisions, to find *their own* ways, to build *their own* future and that of their children, in a rational manner.

THE ORGONOMIC INFANT
RESEARCH CENTER (OIRC)

On December 16, 1949, forty professional people, physicians, nurses, and social workers, met at the Orgone Institute in Forest Hills, New York, to discuss a most difficult task in education: *the study of the healthy child.* They were chosen from among about one hundred workers in the field of orgonomic medicine and education as those probably best suited to approach this task. The newness of the task lay in the facts that "health" in children had come to be a major problem of education, and that the term "healthy child" had never before been clarified; nor had anybody tried to differentiate health from sickness in newborn infants. The complexity of the whole task will emerge clearly from the procedures and developments which took place during the first three months of the actual study of the problem.

Those who are not thoroughly acquainted with the practical aspects of early child-rearing may wonder why and how healthy children can present a problem, and a major problem at that. This question will be answered unequivocally by the events themselves.

The plan was conceived over a period of ten years, from 1939 to 1949, when, finally, the first practical steps toward an organization of the task were taken.

The Orgonomic Infant Research Center (from now on OIRC) was proposed as an organization for research only;

the research would be limited to newborn infants. The task was clarified and confined by the method of exclusion:

• The OIRC would not provide any routine social service which could be provided by other, established child institutions.

• The OIRC would not accept sick children for treatment on a routine basis, except in cases where such treatment would provide important insights for the study of the process of health in newborn infants.

• The OIRC would not engage in sexual or general marriage counseling except for parents whose infants were to be under its care.

These limitations were set for the following reasons:

• Routine services already supplied by other institutions should not be duplicated since this would not serve the main task, which was too big to permit distraction by other educational problems that are well known today and fairly well handled.

• Acceptance of sick children in the OIRC would immediately make necessary the provision of many well-trained child therapists; there are very few well-trained child therapists. Furthermore, the prevalence of infants needing treatment would soon obfuscate the real job—study of the *healthy* child. No profound insights into what constitutes naturally given health in infants were to be expected from the study of the biopathic functions in emotionally sick children. In the course of the past thirty years of psychiatric development no decisive aspects of "health" in children have been obtained. The hope of arriving at sound conclusions about healthy development on the basis of biopathic functions has totally failed. There seems to be no approach to health from the study of sickness. On the other hand, a sounder judgment of sickness was to be expected if it were approached from the standpoint of natural, healthy functioning and judged from this base of operation. However, the base of healthy functioning in newborn infants had to be elaborated before it could become a reliable factor of comparison for the judgment of sickness in children. For example, are whooping cough and constipation naturally given or culturally induced developments? Nobody can tell.

• The training as well as the character of most parents, physicians, and educators is geared to present-day human character structure and social views on education. There can be no disagreement over the fact that emotional diseases in adults are widespread; the average parent, educator, or physician carries the heavy burden of this century's wrong kind of education, which has perpetuated utter ignorance of childhood. The structural distortions in the character of the parents, physicians, and educators are transmitted automatically to the next generation. Thus, the wrong kind of public opinion in education, and with it the warping of the naturally given capacities in the newborn, are reproduced endlessly. Obviously, breaking this vicious circle seemed indispensable. Given our present state of knowledge, this could be accomplished only by the careful choice of the parents whose babies were to be observed and cared for. The choice of suitable parents would in itself present the first major problem to be solved.

Basic Structure of the OIRC

Organization of the OIRC was to reflect the task to be accomplished. In order *to reach the naturally given plasmatic bioenergetic functions of the infant*, the work had to be concentrated on the developmental process from conception through delivery up to the age of about five or six, i.e., the age when the formation of the basic character structure is completed. Accordingly, four major groups had to be established:

1. *Prenatal care of healthy pregnant mothers*

This service was to include sex-economic* counseling of the parents during pregnancy, in particular, regarding orgastic release; routine hygiene measures; removal of common practices which are known to harm the growth of the embryo, such as tight girdles, etc.; use of the orgone accumulator during the entire pregnancy; careful periodic examinations of the bioenergetic behavior of the organism in general and the pelvis in particular. It was to be determined what kind of influence, if any, on embryonic development is exerted by depressions, blocked hatred, crying, etc. We soon learned that almost nothing was known about the emotional factors in pregnancy. We had only a few well-defined clinical experiences at our disposal from which to proceed, such as the blocking of the flow of energy in the organism due to disturbed energy discharge. It was also necessary to find the kind of obstetrician who would not obstruct orgonomic procedures, even if he did not understand them.

2. *Careful supervision of the delivery and the first few days of the newborn's life*

This second task appeared as the most crucial one. Birth and the first few days were well known as the most decisive period of development. Most chronic or melancholic depressions grow out of early frustration; also, the faulty development of perception and its integration during the first six weeks of life were clearly responsible for schizophrenic splits and the schizoid character. During this period

---

* Sex economy refers to the manner in which the organism regulates its biological (orgone) energy.

the pediatric psychiatrist would step in and in cooperation with the mother try to understand the natural expressions of the newborn infant and to remove any obstacles in their way. The greatest difficulty at this time would be the lack of knowledge about the bioenergetic expressions in the newborn infant. *We do not know what the newborn feels or how it experiences its first weeks of life outside the uterus.* We were sure however that with careful observation the problems would turn up rapidly and clearly and would eventually be solved.

3. *Prevention of armoring* during the first five or six years of life*

Here, too, little was known clinically and most of the problems were obscure at the time of our first approach. We could expect that the task of treating children who are already heavily armored would be different from that of recognizing incipient armoring in an otherwise naturally developing child. Nothing was known about which character traits in infancy are due to early armoring and which are due to natural life expression.

In recent years we had seen a few children grow up in an entirely different *self-regulating manner:* children who developed different character reactions. To what extent we were dealing with lawful biological developments remained to be seen. We could find no answers to these questions from any established quarters. We were, therefore, prepared to start from scratch. Only parents, nurses, and pediatricians who had not lost their organ sensation and

---

* The term "armoring" or "armor" refers to the total defense apparatus of the organism, consisting of the rigidities of the character and the chronic spasms of the musculature. Armor functions essentially as a defense against the breakthrough of emotions—primarily anxiety, rage, and sexual excitation.

expression, i.e., their orgonotic sense, would be suitable to
do research in this realm.

4. *Study and recording of the further developments of these children until well after puberty*

This organization of the infant research task precluded
the usual method of setting up a research program and
meeting a deadline. Participants at that first meeting were
repeatedly admonished to be prepared for patient and persistent work over many years and not to expect quick
results; to shed any and every kind of ideal or mystical
expectation regarding "healthy" children or the creation of
"genital characters,"* to be on the lookout for reactions of
disappointment and distress; to learn to recognize mistakes
and wrong ideas about infant upbringing in time; to be
ready to have all personal, structural handicaps brought
freely into the open for thorough discussion; to be willing
to step out of the task if and when they felt inadequate or
impatient; to realize that, practically, we knew nothing
whatsoever about what a "healthy child" is or would turn
out to be.

To see the problems clearly and to formulate them con-
cretely and correctly as they arose would require extremely
slow progress in the development of the project. From ten
to fifteen years of careful work would most probably be
needed to reach the first decisive results on which one could
later safely build. We hoped that these results would make
the great effort worthwhile. It should be kept in mind, however, that the whole project, important as it was, was conceived as a tentative program only. It would not matter
whether or not it was carried out. If it were to fail, we

---

* The term "genital character" is applied to the unneurotic character
structure, which does not suffer from sexual stasis and therefore is capable
of natural self-regulation on the basis of orgastic potency.

would learn why such projects have to fail at this time, and something important would be gained even by a negative outcome.

Professional experience and personal training made every worker in that meeting fully aware of the tremendous consequences of the undertaking. Years of hard work with human character structures had taught us that, quite apart from questions of knowledge and ability, we could not possibly expect armored human beings to deal with the problems of health in a satisfactory manner. Thus, even in the preliminary discussion of the task, we ran into one of the toughest problems to be overcome and solved: Who would be able to handle and accept the work in accordance with the requirements? Would we be able to shed or at least keep in check our own distorted and thwarted structures? Clearly, our handicaps would turn up sooner or later. We did not try in any way to avoid or to hide this major obstacle. On the contrary, only total awareness of our own character structures and willingness to reveal them openly would make it possible for us to proceed. We soon learned that not only was this point of departure correct but also that it was to become the first major insight we gained in this task, a task impossible to perform with human character structures which were obviously thwarted emotionally.

The workers were warned to avoid any kind of gossip, slander, politics; only factual accomplishments would count, and no underhanded activity would be tolerated. Personal ambition and envy of others' accomplishments were to be kept in check. Modesty and fearlessness toward hostile behavior on the part of the haters of childhood were essential requirements.

In order to immediately eliminate any misconception about the nature of the undertaking, it was stated that no public opinion, whatever the source or force, which could impede the development of health in children would be permitted to influence our procedures. No discrimination between mothers who possessed a marriage certificate and others who did not would be tolerated. Religious rituals, such as circumcision, would be judged solely from the standpoint of the good or harm they do to children and not from that of whether or not they are cherished beliefs or customs of groups of people or nations. Furthermore, it was to be clearly understood that whoever felt strongly against natural genital games of three- or five-year-olds, for whatever reasons, should not join in the task. These initial guidelines were necessary to introduce the basic standpoint from which all procedures and judgments would follow.

The human species has for millennia been split into numerous groups according to nationality, race, religion, state, etc. Each group has directed its educational measures toward the adjustments of every new generation to the specific national, religious, or racial ideals and institutions. A dictator, if asked what he thinks a healthy child should be like, would doubtless say he should be a good defender of the honor of the fatherland. A Catholic would claim that a healthy or so-called normal child is one who obeys the customs of Catholicism; killing the "sinful" craving "of the flesh" appears to be the main criterion. The member of Western civilization would define the healthy child as the ideal bearer of Western culture, and the representative of Eastern culture would, by the same token, define health in the child as the ability to be obedient, stoical, unemotional, and fit to carry on the old traditions of the Eastern patriarchate. The official view in dictatorial Russia is that the child "should be like Stalin." We, on the other hand, do not want our children to be like Stalin, or like anybody else for that matter. We want them to be *themselves*.

These few examples make obvious what all these groups have in common: *complete disregard for the nature of the child itself.* Health, normality, fitness are defined according to interests *outside* the sphere of children's development. The child is subjected to the state, as in the dictatorships; or the "culture," as in psychoanalysis; or the Church, or to some historical view, as, for instance, in orthodox Jewish education (circumcision, etc.).

It is not necessary to adduce much proof to refute all these public views in the field of education. They start with what a child SHOULD be or represent, and not with what a newborn child IS. *A newborn child is, first of all, a bit of living nature, an orgonotic system governed by certain bio-energetic laws.* No one will deny the fact that living nature is an infinitely wider realm of existence than the Church, or the state, or the particular culture. If an international brotherhood of men, as the slogan goes, could ever be established on firm ground, this ground could not possibly be a particular state, or church, or culture, or, for that matter, any goal or idea which lies outside the functioning of a newborn child. If a natural basis for international cooperative functioning of society were ever given, it is the living principle which each newborn child brings with it, be it in Leningrad, Lhasa, or New York. Modern sociological research has convinced us beyond any doubt that the newborn generation brings with it only the *bioenergetic* heritage and nothing else—no culture, no religion, no citizenship, not even an absolute, inborn love for its own mothers.

Now, instead of adapting social conditions to the living principle in newborn children; instead of developing all cultural ideals toward the preservation and security of the living principle inborn in the child, the child is being adapted to the particular church, state, or culture. Whereas nature tends to unite mankind in the deep resources of the living principle, the cultural, religious, state, and other principles tend automatically to disrupt and to split this basic unity of international human existence. This should be easy to understand in the United States, where the melting together of national, cultural, and religious principles is a specific characteristic. It will be more difficult to understand in countries where national restrictiveness due to language or history tends to separate the nation from the world at large.

The living principle is not only much broader and deeper than any other principle of education; it clearly directs our views toward the central goal of preventive mental hygiene in a quite natural way. It is necessary to explain this statement at some length, since it might astonish many readers, though it is simple and matter-of-fact.

The generally valid conclusion which can be derived from our characterological knowledge is this: If the rigid armoring of the human animal is the basic common principle of all his emotional misery; if it is this armoring which puts him, alone among biological species, beyond the pale of natural functioning, then it follows logically that *prevention of rigid armoring is the main and central goal of preventive mental hygiene.*

The ease with which the unarmored human being is able to cope with life's difficulties is another proof of the correctness of this contention. The biophysical principle which is so overpowering compared with any other point of view seems not to be denied by reason or true religion (apart from the Church business), and it is supported by every major event in the history of man. Yet this principle has been replaced over the millennia by the narrower ones which leave the inborn nature of the child completely out of the picture. There must be some important reason for this.

Prevention of armoring would not appear necessary if our children could grow up as nature or "God" has prescribed. It has been firmly established that organisms which function according to the law of nature are free of biopathies.*
The history of the human race is full of statements by great explorers and sages which corroborate this simple fact. However, before the discovery of the organismic orgone energy nobody knew what the "law of nature" looked like exactly. Like other animals, children are born everywhere without armoring. This constitutes the firmest foundation of mental hygiene, far better than any attempts at a later date to disarmor the human animal or to prevent armoring. Yet, this natural principle is continuously drowned out by other views which make it ineffective. We must ask how this could happen. There are several ways:

1. The natural bioenergetic principle in the newborn baby is systematically smothered and ruined by the armored parent and educator, who in turn are supported in their ignorance by powerful social institutions which thrive on the armoring of the human animal.

2. A simple but tenacious misinterpretation of nature governs all education and cultural philosophy. It is the idea that nature and culture are incompatible. In accordance with this "cultural" ideology, psychoanalysts have failed to distinguish between primary natural and secondary perverse, cruel drives, and they are continuously killing nature in the newborn while they try to extinguish the "brutish little animal." They are completely ignorant of the fact that it is *exactly this killing of the natural principle which creates the secondary perverse and cruel nature,* human nature so called, and that these artificial cultural creations

* "Biopathy" refers to all disease processes caused by a dysfunction in the autonomic life apparatus. See *The Cancer Biopathy*, Farrar, Straus & Giroux, New York, 1973.—*Eds.*

in turn make compulsive moralism and brutal laws necessary.

3. Since, at present, most of the human race is distinguished from the rest of the animal kingdom by rigid armoring; since, furthermore, the great longing for redemption is a clear expression of the longing for a re-establishment of the unarmored, natural state ("paradise"); since, finally, the armored animal, man, is utterly incapable of reaching his most ardently longed-for goal, namely, freedom of his organism from rigidity, dullness, immobility, and the rest of the biophysical straitjacket, he must of necessity fear and hate it; and the less he is capable of reaching it the more he must hate it. This is the crux of what we term "emotional plague." Therefore, the smothering of nature in the child is not done merely to adapt it to some state or church or culture; this is a secondary function. Primarily, it is the terror that strikes the armored human being when he faces any kind of living expression that is responsible for the systematic armoring of newborn generations. *It is brutal hate, based on terror, which regulates the armoring of the newborn.*

Seen from this biophysical vantage point, the adaptation to culture, state, or church is merely a result, albeit a highly praised and powerful means of evading the only type of functioning which could and will, sooner or later, resolve man's misery in a simple fashion. Institutions of society which require the smothering of nature in the child and his adaptation to ideals which are foreign to his nature, are secondary, insignificant functions, if seen from the standpoint of the *living* principle. Institutions and ideologies are within man's power to change, if he wished to do so. The biophysical basis is beyond it. He knows this when he says that "God" is beyond his reach. The idea that God cannot be recognized or touched is a clear expression of man's inability to reach the biological core of his total existence. He has entangled himself in ideas which resulted from his first denial of nature ("original sin"), and he finds himself bound up in a maze of words which lead away from the truth; in ideas which have no meaning; in cruel deeds he abhors and yet commits, as if forced to do so by evil fate ("the devil").

The study of "human nature" during the last few decades has clarified so much. We know now, in a very practical manner, that man's cruelty is directed mainly against what he most longs for. With every attempt to reach his deeply felt, holy goal, he meets nothing but his own rigidity. *In the repeated, desperate attempts to break through this rigidity every love impulse changes into hate.* Man does not want to hate; he is forced to hate by his armoring. It is clearer now why the more he speaks of "peace," the more surely he gets war.

It is also clear why man kills nature in every newborn child and, with it, the only hope for a solution of his main troubles. He kills it with a consistency and an intricate machinery of ideas and institutions, evasions and erroneous beliefs. If his efforts were only used in the right way, they could move mountains.

I have described extensively in other publications what I have sketched here in a few pages. However, no one has tried as yet to sketch the nature of what we call a "healthy child," as seen from the biophysical viewpoint only.

During the past few years, we have had the opportunity to observe the development of children, from birth through a period of about four to five years, who were not, to the extent possible, impeded in their growth by any considerations of culture, church, or state. Let us summarize briefly what we learned. We do not claim to present a complete picture of this new and unusual experience. These children were the best teachers we have ever had; they taught us more about biology and self-regulation than we had ever hoped to learn in thirty years of work as psychiatrists and physicians. It was like looking into the "promised land." It also was a lesson in what man's emotional plague does to him.

If no severe damage has already been inflicted on it in the womb, the newborn infant brings with it all the richness of natural plasticity and development. This infant is not, as so many erroneously believe, an empty sack or a chemical machine into which everybody and anybody can pour his or her special ideas of what a human being ought to be. It brings with it an enormously productive and adaptive energy system which, out of its own resources, will make contact with its environment and *begin to shape that environment according to its needs.* The basic task of all education, directed by interest in the child and not by interest in party programs, profit, church, etc., is to remove every obstacle in the way of this naturally given productivity and plasticity of the biological energy. Here, for the first time, we have found a positive and broad base of operation. These children will have to choose their own ways and determine their own fates. We must learn from them instead of forcing upon them our own cockeyed ideas and malicious practices, which have been shown in every new generation to be most damaging and ridiculous. LET THE CHILDREN THEMSELVES DECIDE THEIR OWN FUTURE. Our task is to protect their natural powers to do so.

It is logical, therefore, to examine the bioenergetic motility of all participants in this project, and their readiness to step aside and, for once, let *nature* speak. It is easy to call humanity "back to nature." It is hard to stop interfering with it.

To the physician or educator who has dealt with man's

biopathic misery over decades, it was self-evident that sooner or later, in one form or another, our project would meet with the same intense anxiety and brutal hatred which is so well known from medical practice with individuals, as well as from the mass slaughters by Hitlerian lunatics. However, to those gathered in that room in Forest Hills it must have sounded peculiar and even strange when I sharply pointed out that terrific obstacles were to be expected in their own midst, that no human character structure which had been molded during the past few thousand years is free or could ever fully free itself of this *hatred toward the living.* We should have no illusions. This deep structural hatred, no matter how well covered up by love and interest in the child, would inevitably turn up and try to kill the OIRC.

It was decided not to go to the public with the new experiences but to wait patiently until enough had been learned about the reactions of the research center to the coming disclosures. Before anybody could hope to do anything of real significance in public, he would have to learn to recognize the hatred against the living in its hidden and devious ways and to find adequate means of coping with it.

After these preparatory sketches of the terrain, we proceeded to discuss organizational matters. The first step was to be the demonstration of armoring in biopathic children and first signs of armoring in fairly healthy children.

Problems of Healthy Children
during the First Puberty
(Ages Three to Six)

The problems entailed in rearing healthy children were encountered right at the beginning of the OIRC, when I faced the task of presenting David, the son of a physician, to the workers. Demonstrating a lively, spontaneous boy of six would seem only to provide a pleasurable experience for everyone, a respite from the drudgery of biopathology. Why then did I feel worried and hesitant? I knew that this task required complete honesty, but thousands of honest people had come out with the truth about children and love and life, from Pestalozzi to Freud, Neill, and so many others. Honesty was at work in hundreds of attempts to get at the basic trouble in education, yet not one of these attempts had succeeded. Thus, honesty and obvious facts alone were not sufficient. Doubtless there was a barrier against all such attempts which no one had ever been able to surmount; the existence of such a barrier had never even been mentioned. It is true that writers, philosophers, and poets had complained about the depravity of "human nature" and described the eternal struggle against "evil." But this same human nature and evil seemed to be conceived of as immutable, eternal. Nowhere was there an indication of a possible connection between so-called evil human nature and the fact that all attempts to get at the obvious in life, love, and childhood had failed so miserably.

In those days, before the first child demonstration, I felt I was looking into a dense fog which hid the solution to the greatest riddle confronting mankind: *Why had nobody as yet spoken about the obvious?*

It was clear that this fog was concealing access to the solution of the riddle. Could it be that the fog was not naturally given, "just" ignorance, or "just" human nature, or "just" human malice, or "just" this, or "just" that, but that it was a smoke screen deliberately laid out to blur the view?

Probably the "fog" had somehow grown out of man's fear of the living. But how? What were the links which led from this fear to the dense fog which hung like a veil over anything worth knowing? There was no immediate answer. And it was useless to try to lift a fog if you did not know how it had come about and what had kept it there, hiding the riddles of life from man's view for thousands of years. If the fog had anything at all to do with man's fear of the living, the fear I had found in biopathic patients, then this fear-hatred would inevitably turn up in the course of events and, possibly, some of the connecting links between it and the fog would become clear.

In order to obtain reliable results from this infant research, it would be necessary to keep the "fog" from penetrating into the OIRC and preventing the first true glimpses into the well-hidden territory. Here my biopsychiatric experience was helpful. I knew that the average human being employs, purely structurally, certain techniques to escape from the essential in everything pertaining to problems of the living. If it were possible to keep only a few of these human techniques of evasion out of the OIRC, a wedge could be driven into the flexible yet solid wall of fog that hung in front of the simple and obvious. With the first rock-bottom results thus achieved, even if they were minute, there would be hope of driving the wedge deeper into the foggy, muggy, swamp-like veil. This was no more than a hope, and a very shaky one at that. If it were easy to penetrate the fog, one or another among hundreds of great explorers who toiled during the past three or four millennia of mystical patriarchy would have succeeded.

I was very discouraged in those days before the demonstration and clung with all my vigor to the few safeguards against failure which were at my disposal:

1. I would overcome the taboo, which exists generally, against discussing matters of genitality freely and frankly in public, as I had done twenty years ago in Austria and Germany. Children's genitality would be handled just as openly as any other subject.

2. The taboo against touching the human body while dealing with emotional matters would also have to be done away with. Psychoanalysts had strictly introduced this into education and medicine, protecting themselves against the severe emotional impact of living processes. It had already been eliminated in the medical orgone therapy of adults. Now it had to be removed from education. Educators who deal with children, and mothers who rear them, would have to learn how to handle infant bodies without fear and emotional disgust. They would have to learn to become first-aid workers in education.

I had always felt that the educator had failed somehow to find his place in the general social task, like a physician or a technician. The pediatrician had to be called when a child got constipated. Why should not the mother or the nursery school teacher be able to handle an acute constipation due to bioenergetic, emotional blocking of the peristalsis in the intestines? Just as a physician is called when a leg has been broken, it should be possible to call an educator into the home when a child of two gets into a fit of rage with which the mother cannot cope. Today's educator knows more about such matters than does the pediatrician, who has learned nothing about them in medical school. The mother and the educator are the naturally given persons to deal with such emergencies. Would it be possible to teach mothers and educators to remove an acute block in the throat or in the diaphragm whenever it developed? Thus, chronic armoring could be successfully prevented by persons who are always near the child.

3. The next taboo to be broken by all means was that against revealing one's own mistakes and shortcomings. Without perfect frankness about our own weaknesses there is no hope of ever piercing the fog. Physicians or teachers who strut along the road of professional life exhibiting their "faultlessness" and their "perfect" accomplishment are, to put it bluntly, completely worthless in such pioneering work. I doubt that they are of much use in routine work, either. Our workers would have to be convinced that to see and to clarify (not to "admit") a mistake is the only true way to learn to do better on the next occasion. And the mistakes would have to include those made in educating our own children. David, whom I was to demonstrate, was one of those children.

David had been asked a few days before the demonstration whether he would be willing to show the doctors and teachers his body and where "it gets stuck," as he calls it. He was not only willing but eager to do so.

Since demonstrations of children before large groups of listeners, and with such highly emotional subjects as "belly feelings," "playing doctor," playing with the genitals, etc., had never before been attempted, scarcely anything was known about possible reactions on the part of the child or the audience. However, a beginning had to be made some-where. David was present, facing the audience, when his story was told.

When David was born it had been clear to his parents that armoring of the organism would have to be prevented. However, no one knew in what form initial armoring would appear, whether it would be possible to recognize it in time, what kind of procedures would have to be employed to dissolve the first blockings, and what the result would be.

It was stressed at the meeting that progress could be expected only from candid admission of the fact that noth-ing whatsoever was known about prevention of armoring: how much of it would have to be accomplished by the right kind of upbringing and how much would have to be dealt with by therapy. The task was compared with that of putting a railroad across a mountain range. The access was known, but the details of the terrain were not, and each curve or grade would have to be studied as we ad-vanced. The importance of this basic approach was stressed repeatedly; there is no greater obstacle to unprejudiced inquiry than ready-made answers to unknown problems.

The period of six years, from birth to the day of the demonstration, was characterized by an intense and con-tinuous struggle on the part of David's parents to recognize the onset of armoring in the child's organism in time and to find the proper approach to dissolve it. Since the child lived not only in the family but was also exposed to the influences of school and community, rather involved situa-tions often arose.

The main result of the struggle to bring up David in a self-regulatory manner was that no chronic armoring had developed. This was made possible only by a continuous alertness to certain danger spots where tendencies to chronic armoring were recurring in a typical way.

Let us first survey the positive results of this self-regulatory upbringing.

The child had not developed the dysfunctions so typical of children who are brought up in the "usual" "orderly" way.

His body was soft; it yielded easily to any kind of passive movement. There was no rigidity, apart from some restriction in the pelvis, which will be discussed later. His skin was warm and radiated orgonotic heat, particularly in the region of the solar plexus. His parents reported that when he slept his ears became red and his face strongly flushed. His gait was coordinated, soft and yielding. There was no imbalance; he caught his balance easily when he tripped. He ran well and was very active most of the time.

David gave freely, shared what he had, but got desperate when other children only took from him without responding to his kindness. Even as a small child he used to share things with his parents or other children. He was not taught to do so; these qualities developed quite spontaneously. We may assume with some certainty that an organism which yields to its natural emotions is also inclined to be outgoing in other respects. The parents admitted they had often wondered and worried about how this yielding attitude would affect his later existence when he met the "take, hit, and run" attitude of armored character structures.

David was social to a very high degree; he got along with nearly everyone and made friends easily. On the other hand, he disliked noise and roughness intensely. He often complained that there was too much noise in the school he attended at the time of the demonstration. He also liked to withdraw into a corner or into his room "in order to think and be by myself." He could get very angry. This was likely to happen when he wanted something badly and no explanation was given to him why he could not have it. On the other hand, he was not greedy or possessive and waited patiently until he got what had been promised to him. When he was five years old, he wanted a two-wheel bicycle, the type he had seen other children with. When it was explained to him that he would get one when he reached the age of six or seven, he waited very patiently, only occasionally asking whether he would definitely get the bicycle at seven; also, how long he had to wait, i.e., how long was two years. There was no impatience in his asking, only matter-of-fact inquiry. The parents were very careful not to disappoint David, and to keep their promises to him. This produced a deep trust in his parents' behavior; he was never cheated in anything. He learned about the creation and birth of children in his fourth year and, from time to time, would ask some other deep question, which was answered faithfully and truthfully. We shall return to this in a short while to show where and how the armored world interfered with this natural development.

David's emotions flowed freely. He was afraid when fear was rational; he hated when hate was appropriate; and he loved with a beautiful abundance when love was wanted and freely given.

He also could be irrational, cranky, and "nasty." We shall later see under which circumstances rational turns into irrational behavior.

Usually, his eyes were moist, very expressive, and sparkling. At times, however, they became dull, "flat," and inexpressive. His parents slowly learned to understand how his eyes lost their deep, sparkling expression and turned dull.

The naturally given health in David could well be described in terms of what kind of common children's troubles he did *not* develop; troubles which in most of the psychiatric and educational literature are either taken for granted as physiological accompaniments of the child's development or are not considered much of a problem. It should be stated most emphatically that observation of the healthy child's development was directed among other things by the knowledge that later severe biopathic derangements have their roots in such unrecognized "normal" troubles in small children. As I said before, we must shed any preconceived ideas about what is "normal" or "abnormal" in a child before getting at the problem of health.

David was never constipated. His bowel movements were regular and full, and there was never any fuss about them whatsoever. Very rarely diarrhea might set in when he ate too much fruit or similar food. But there was no "anal" complication. Neither was he in any way taught to be regular or clean. He showed repugnance to excretions of his own accord. This fact is in agreement with the natural cleanliness seen in dogs, cats, research mice, etc. Thus tales about "natural, inherited" liking for fecal pleasures turn out to be a myth, which came about because psychoanalysis derived its observations from *armored* character structures and mistook secondary drives for naturally given tendencies. This mistake led to the notion that the child is born with inclinations toward dirtiness and has to "sublimate" its pregenital anal desires. The observations were correct, but they pertained only to already distorted human structures. And the distortions usually set in right after birth, if not in the uterine existence. What has been said here about anal tendencies is valid for many other traits. We must, therefore, make an entirely new start in

judging infantile behavior by distinguishing what is naturally given, i.e., primary drives, from what is the result
of the warping of primary drives, i.e., secondary drives.

David's father and mother had never observed any
sadistic inclinations in him. They reported that he could
be rough and tough; he would hit them in anger when he
felt wronged; but he never pinched merely for fun; he
never tortured flies or other animals; he never enjoyed
bullying or maltreating other children; and he never was
destructive for the sake of destructiveness alone. On the
contrary, he was always very unhappy when he broke a
vase or a plate, though he was never reprimanded for
breaking something by accident and was carefully kept
away from anything that could implant feelings of guilt.

The subject of infantile destructiveness is of such paramount importance because on its evaluation depend our
views of the origin of human destructiveness and the educational and social measures to be taken against it.

The old schools of education, which rely so heavily
on the assumption of inborn "bad instincts" that must be
curbed by law and punishment, have nothing whatsoever
to contribute to the solution of the problem of the healthy
child. They are a major characteristic of the "generation
that failed." If everything is inborn, then nothing but
punishment can help. Unfortunately, there are rational
reasons why the police departments of this world adhere
to the hereditary rather than to the environmental point
of view. The law is *necessary* in the face of the amount of
destructiveness in the human animal. What we object to
is not the existence of the law and of punishment. We
know better than those who punish blindly whence stems
the necessity of the law, irrational in long-range terms as
it may be. What we object to is the reluctance of the law
to help change things so that not more but less and less

law is necessary. We object to the stupidity and cruelty of the same human character structures which seize upon existing laws and apply them mechanically, blindly, recklessly, and cruelly, with no regard to the problems involved of preventing crime and with utter disrespect for any kind of decency in the search for improvement. This is the result of the mechanization of the human mind. Once a pattern has been formed, the mechanistic human structure remains stuck in it and proceeds like a mechanical monster, obstructing the very ideals it is so prone to proclaim on the anniversaries of the American, Russian, French, and other revolutions.

We shall return to this mechanized functioning in other equally important contexts. Now let us return to David. *He had not developed any kind of sadism.* This, of course, is a major event in the history of the human race, no matter whether anyone pays attention to it now or not. It will in due time be of an infinitely greater importance than any of the present-day resolutions to establish peace on this earth. The peace resolutions are, at best, no more than desperate attempts at curbing political malignancy, and they probably are the *worst* means of cheating people out of peaceful lives in the interests of political power machines. On the other hand, knowledge of how to prevent the development of sadism in our children would make most of the campaigning for peace unnecessary. *There would be no secondary-drive structure in the human animal on which to build for wars.*

His parents reported that although David was not sadistic he could hate very fiercely. He disliked people who had no contact or who showed false contact. He would refuse to go near them, to greet them, or to be friendly with them. This characteristic was also seen in a few other self-regulated children who grew up in our circle.

At times the kind of immediate contact David was able to make with people he liked was astonishing. Someone once called this perfect contact "transparence." This is a very good term, and I suggest that it be adopted to describe a kind of simple behavior which is immediate, fully in contact, and lucid, with no hidden motives or veiled attitudes. "Transparence" is a good word to describe the character structure which displays natural honesty, frankness, directness, contact, humility, and friendliness. We had seen these qualities emerge from the depth of biopathic people. Now we meet them in naturally growing children. They are there; they do not have to be taught. A wonderful possibility opens up with this fact.

David had not been circumcised. His parents did not feel that they should submit to a cruel custom introduced and spread over the ages by a people in distress. It did not matter that the medical profession had taken over this cruel custom under pseudo-hygienic pretexts. What mattered was that the parents did not want to inflict a painful injury on a newborn baby.

"Why do they cut off the little skin from the weewees?" David asked when he was three. He was told that some 5,000 years ago the Jews had thought they could be different from other people and serve their God better if they cut the skins off the genitals of their male children. They thought it would make them cleaner. But, David was told, you can keep your penis clean without having the foreskin cut away, simply by washing it daily. He had learned to retract his foreskin and to clean the glans with no shame or hesitation whatsoever.

The child grew up without having nightmares and anxiety dreams. Thus, anxiety in children is *not* a natural development, as claimed by some psychoanalytic schools. It is not true that the child's ego is by its very nature in-

capable of coping with emotions and bioenergetic excita-
tions. In a healthy child the ego develops with the emotions; it is not set against them. It has developed the
capacity to accept and carry whatever emotions exist and
is merely the regulator and executor of the bioenergetic
shifts.

On the other hand, it is also untrue that healthy children have no anxiety. They have anxiety at times, as do all
living creatures. The view that health is something absolutely "perfect," that a "healthy" child "should not have"
this or that, has nothing to do with reality or with reason.
It is clearly a mystical redemption fantasy of neurotic
structures to expect the perfect and the absolute. The difference between healthy and sick children lies not in the
fact that the former have no emotional disturbances and
the latter have; it is determined by the *capacity of the
child to get out of the acute biopathic entanglement and
not to get stuck in it for a lifetime,* as do typically neurotic
children. The difference lies in whether or not a background for biopathic functions and symptoms has developed. Here the great importance of the "character neurotic
reaction basis"* reveals itself. What counts is not the iso-
lated acute symptomatic attack but the character structure
underlying it. If there is no basic warping of the bioenergetic structure in the child from conception onward, the
acute anxiety or irrational hate attacks will have no soil in
which to take root and thus to become chronic biopathic
character traits. As was so amply proven by character
analytic investigations, the healthy and the sick are not
distinguished by the ideas or the emotions which an organism develops but solely by the total economy of the bioenergy system. If there is an undischargeable surplus of

---

* Cf. Reich, *Character Analysis*, 3rd ed., Ch. VIII, pp. 185 ff.

bioenergy, the most innocent ideas and emotions will become pathogenic and feed on the energy stasis. If there is no stasis, the most dangerous emotions and ideas will be rendered harmless.

David's father said that David often told him: "I'll kill you if you don't do" this or that; but there was no force behind it, and these ideas vanished as quickly as they had appeared. On the other hand, a boy who is highly charged emotionally may *mean* it if he tells his father that he might kill him. In the child with frustrated bioenergy, even as seemingly harmless an idea as, for example, pinching the father's nose will have the intent of murder.

It is, therefore, the background of the psychic functions, and not the psychic content itself, that counts. David's parents found this out when he began to develop a great urge to play cowboy. For months on end, he would run around with his two guns blazing, shooting to death everybody in his way. Years ago his parents would have adhered to the absolute ideas of what a child should and should not have or play. For a child to play with guns was deeply abhorred and feared. It was thought that such games would necessarily warp the character structure. Experience showed this was not the case. As the months of gun play passed, David's parents began to feel that there was nothing in the background to structuralize an impulse to shoot. They felt that his playing with guns would slowly subside. And so it did. David lost all interest in guns, and at the time of the demonstration, I was told he preferred to build with bricks.

These insights are new and of extreme importance. The emphasis on the prevention of biopathies, including severe antisocial drives, shifts from what a child does or speaks or thinks to the emotional structure which does it. There is no reason to worry when a child like David says he will kill you, or when he actually picks up a knife and acts as if he was going to use it. On the other hand, there is all the reason in the world to worry if a child is always polite and obedient, never threatens to kill, but in its characterological structure harbors intense murder fantasies or develops phobias about knives and murder. The first child will never commit a murder, whereas the second will possibly or even probably develop a structure which all through its lifetime will have to ward off murder impulses or which will, under given circumstances, actually commit murder. It is well known that many murderers are polite sneaks, characterologically speaking. Think here of the sneak character of a Himmler or Stalin.

Peculiar as this kind of reasoning may still seem, it becomes a matter of course once one has had enough experience and learned to recognize and comprehend the structural realities that develop in childhood. The task of preventive education becomes much simpler. We do not have to watch every one of the child's millions of thoughts. What we have to do is keep the child's biosystem free of any tendency toward stasis of its biological energy, observable in frustration. The rest will take care of itself. In this manner, the bioenergetic point of view makes it possible to solve the problem of structuralization, inaccessible to psychology, which deals with ideas only. It is, to repeat, the energy charge accompanying the ideas, and not the ideas themselves, which counts. Pathological ideas collapse like a house of cards if there is no stasis of bioenergy for them to feed on.

This bioenergetic view also relieves much of our worry about bad influences which are exerted on our children by greedy, reckless, stupid business enterprises which take into account only money and never the child's welfare. A child who is healthy in our sense, i.e., who is lacking the background for pathological developments, will not be harmed by violence in movies or comic books. He will either show no interest in these cruelties or will react with disgust, or will pick them up for a while and then drop them again. The sick child will eagerly soak up the cruelty, embody it in his structure, add to it from his own fantasy life, and carry it to evil perfection by one of the many devious, hidden ways in which the emotional plague operates. He will pull out the wings of living flies slowly, with conscious delight in the inflicted pain, fantasizing that he is killing his father or teacher. He will create monsters in his fantasy which will do the evil job while the dreamer stands aside, innocently and cowardly. He will pinch puppies, or pull the tails of cats. Later, as a grownup, he will shoot trusting deer in front of the headlights of his car; he will for hours on end catch fish, not to eat them, but to torture them by pulling out the hook sharply and painfully; he will, in brief, become a perfect Hitlerian killer.

In David, the first indications of a destructive (not sadistic) trait were clearly discerned by his parents when he entered his first puberty, around three years of age, and failed to make a smooth adjustment to his genital urges. Much more was learned about the problem of the healthy child during the period of trouble that followed than during the whole preceding time, which had been comparatively smooth.

The troubles David had between his third and the first half of his sixth year completely destroyed the idea that a healthy child is never emotionally upset. It was learned that health consists not in the total absence of sickness but in the ability of the organism to overcome sickness and to emerge basically unhurt.

It was further learned that, next to the period immediately after birth, the period of genital development ("first puberty") is the most crucial one. What occurred during this period confirmed the important findings which have been made by character analytic investigation of sick adults.

The experiences of this same period demonstrated the utter inadequacy of the common ideas of education, such as "Give the boy sex information when he is twelve years old," or "Do not tell the child more than he asks for." It was learned that all such rules are no more than protective devices used by grownups to make themselves appear modern regarding sex education and at the same time to help them avoid touching the "hot potato." First, any kind of "sex education" always comes too late. Second, one cannot "educate" about sex as you educate in reading. The term is without meaning. What one can do is to help the child overcome its emotional, bioenergetic problems. Third, the child's biological development depends almost entirely on the manner in which it has grown from the prenatal period into the first puberty. It appeared senseless to speak of "giving sex information" to children who never had occasion to see spontaneous mating in nature. It also appeared perfectly senseless to "give sex education," while at the same time letting the world of sex neurotics influence the child's environment. It is by no means enough to give sex information; the child must be actively protected against the evil ideas and practices of the sex neurotics who have grown up in the first half of this century. And, finally, no mere talking about sex can ever solve the problem. *The child must* LIVE *its nature practically and fully.*

As recently as twenty or twenty-five years ago, printing such statements would have and actually did provoke social ostracism. Today things are better, but far from sufficiently adjusted to the child's needs. We shall soon see what it actually means to have one's child "live its nature fully." We shall also see how far removed the idea of "natural self-regulation" is from the reality of infancy and early childhood. If we refuse to recognize the wide gap, it is in order to save ourselves the shame which comes with the realization of where we are with our glib talk and where nature is.

I have had to confess to myself that after thirty years of psychiatric work and study, I really knew very little about childhood.

When we speak of the totality or the "wholeness" of the biosystem, we mean something very practical. It is not only the totality of the organism at each moment of existence, not only the "red thread" that runs through all developments, connecting the present with the most distant past; it is the complete harmony of the child with its environment. Accordingly, it is impossible to have healthy children growing in a sick environment. It means, furthermore, that under no circumstances can we expect to jump suddenly from a sick past into a healthy future. It will take several generations of newborn infants growing up under an ever-widening horizon of knowledge of the child's true nature before the first signs of the world of the Children of the Future begin to appear.

It is not the inborn nature of the child that constitutes the difficulty. The trouble lies in the thinking and acting of the majority of educators, parents, and physicians. It lies in the maze of wrong opinions which have nothing to do with the child. It lies in the fact that, at present, social interest, as represented by newspapers, magazines, etc., with very few exceptions, is completely centered on diplomatic maneuvering and not on our single most important hope: the child.

We have learned that instead of a jump into the realm of the Children of the Future, we can hope for no more than a steady advance, in which the healthy new overlaps the sick old structure, with the new slowly outgrowing the old. Any other expectation will only lead to disappointment and discouragement. It will only encourage the enemies of childhood—the politician, the party member, and the like—to say triumphantly: We always told you so; nothing can be done about it. Stick to good old politics.

The slowness of change will have to be accompanied by firmness of conviction and the resolution not to permit any antichild attitudes to interfere with the development. This means that, to begin with, it would be of much greater importance to prepare carefully than to rush ahead unprepared, only to retreat later in utter defeat. These things must be stated repeatedly, since the inclination of the present-day human structure to reach results quickly and at the lowest cost in exertion, to hail instead of to know, to run away as soon as the first real obstacles are met, is so very great. One can enjoy the first real fruits of one's efforts; one can be thrilled by the first glimpses into the realm of the Children of the Future *only* if one has learned fully how to become aware of and how to overcome the tremendous obstacles in the way. It is wiser to build one's bridge carefully and not to take a single step before it is safe to proceed. Only a foundation of rock will do, not sand.

David's troubles began when, at three years old, after a bath, he developed a falling anxiety and suffered the first major disaster in his structural development.* The shock-like holding of his breath during the experience of falling had left a deep imprint on his structure, despite the fact that he did not, as do other, unattended children, develop a chronic biopathic contraction in his throat around this first injury. The emotional scar, thus embedded, would

* See pp. 114–35.

from then on turn up with a machine-like precision when-ever and wherever the child became entangled emotionally in an irrational manner. The scar was not active during the first two years of his life. Only occasionally, when he fell and hurt himself badly or was frightened by one thing or another, would his respiration stop, and he would for a while be unable to exhale. However, when he entered his first puberty, the emotional scar would become more apparent.

The trouble that began to develop at the end of his third year was basically centered on his genital develop-ment. David did not show any tendency, as most children do, to ask innumerable, seemingly senseless, compulsively repetitive questions about all kinds of irrelevant things. It had been suspected for a long time in character-analytic work that such questions were due to a repression of the one basic question about where children come from, how they get into the mother. Since such information was care-fully kept from growing children the genuine urge to know was blocked and replaced by bursts of irrelevant inquiry. David's questions had always been answered in a matter-of-fact manner. That infants grow in the mother's belly was no problem at all for him. Even at two and one-half years of age he had indicated wonderment about how they got into the mother. He was told the truth in a simple way. He used to speak freely about the sexual relations of his parents and of other people. Once, he asked whether it would be possible for him to sleep with his mother and for his father to sleep with his nursemaid. There was no trace of smutty curiosity or pathological eagerness in this ques-tion. He was told truthfully that people live with and embrace their wives or husbands, and that when he grew up he would have a girl too whom he would love, embrace, and eventually have children with. He was pleased at the prospect and began to look forward to growing up and having a girl of his own. Here it was learned in actual experience what previously had been only surmised from work on sick adults, namely, that a pathological mother fixation in a boy does not develop unless the way to other partners has been blocked. David's parents said that he never showed the type of mother fixation which is so typical in children growing up in the usual way. He did not cry if his mother left for the evening; he would not cling to her in a sticky manner. He never demanded love in an unreasonable way, since he was given love whenever he needed it. His parents never saw any kind of pathological sexual curiosity in him. He never peeped furtively into windows behind which women undressed, as other boys do, or tried to look under a skirt to catch a glimpse of the female genitals. It should be emphasized that he had never been told not to do such things. He simply did not do them. This again confirms the sex-economic premise that such behavior is not natural but the result of suppression of the primary natural drives.

David had been drinking from the bottle up to age three, and made the transition from the oral to the genital phase easily and without any disturbance. His speech was developing perfectly, with clear diction and distinct wording. His parents experienced great pleasure watching him pick up new words easily and incorporate them into his vocabulary.

In a quite natural fashion David began to turn to little girls when he was about three. He established a warm friendship with a little girl one year older than he who lived nearby. They were together most of the time, hiding sometimes. The parents knew that they had begun to investigate each other sexually.

At three and one-half years of age, a slight phobic idea

made its first appearance. David had established the habit
of "having a talk" with his father. He used to say, "I want
to talk things over with you." His father then took him
into the car and drove to whatever place the child designated. They would sit on the grass and he would start
asking questions. He had begun to ask reasoned questions
about "how things are made" at a very early age. Nobody
had ever tried to induce such interest. One day he asked
why women had hair at their genitals. What was the hair
for? The questions sounded slightly queer, not quite like
the usual David. He was told that hair appears at the
genitals in both men and women when they grow up, and
that he too would have hair there. David's father thought
that David had examined the little girl's vaginal opening
and had wondered why she didn't have hair like his mother.

A while later he came back with some other questions:
Why do girls have a little opening and why is it red? He
was told that the opening is for receiving the male organ
when the girl grew up and that children came out from
there. However, this rational question and answer did not
quite touch the real thing David wanted to know. From
his questions it appeared that the "red" had somewhat
disturbed him.

We know today what was so bitterly fought and slan-
dered some thirty years ago, namely, that he was bothered
about the "cut" in girls. He did not express it openly, and
his father did not try to penetrate deeper but waited for it
to mature. Around such apparently "innocent" questions
castration anxiety usually develops later.

Before going further into the preventive measures taken
against persistence of armoring, we must become fully
aware of the wide implications involved.

What orgonomy calls the "core functions" of the organism were not accessible either to medicine or to education before the discovery of *armor* and the clear distinction of primary and secondary drives. We now know how the armoring of the human animal splits the organism into a bad, sinful reality—the devil—and a moral demand—the good—which eternally, but vainly, tries to overcome the bad. Orgonomy is not in disagreement with anyone about the demands made generally regarding decency, truthfulness, politeness, kindness, cooperation, and tolerance. There is not and cannot be any quarrel about the desirability of these human qualities and their great importance for the welfare of human existence. What orgonomy contests, on the basis of clear-cut medical and educational experience, is the possibility of ever attaining these objectives by any kind of compulsive or purely ethical norms. It is one of the human animal's great tragedies that it has set up these ideals as the goals to be striven for, as the highest aims of civilized life, but at the same time, it has completely blocked the way to their achievement. It is equally tragic that human cultures based entirely on the belief in man's dignity and his basic decency should in such a disastrous manner have blocked off and opposed free development of the very qualities in newborn infants which are the natural carriers of the high-minded, ethical demands. Orgonomy disagrees with the established view when faced with the question of how to make the ideal demands a reality on which to safely build human social cooperation. Those who operate with "thou shalt" and "thou shalt not" somehow have no inkling of the *inborn* moral behavior in man. The orgonomic principle of self-regulation relies fully on the natural structure of the newborn infant, and with good reason. If you let your child grow as nature has created it, if you do not warp its basic needs into anti-natural, asocial drives, the so-called secondary drives, then no compulsive suppression of "badness" will be necessary; the vicious circle of strict morals and bad nature will cease to exist and to mar human lives. The eternal expelling of the devil has so thoroughly failed because the natural needs, especially the sexual ones, have been suppressed, creating the secondary, asocial, criminal drives which, of course, *must* be suppressed. They must be suppressed morally because, unlike other social needs, they do not regulate themselves, since they are *not* natural. After the antisocial in the human animal has been created, the fight against it then becomes hopeless if authoritarian moralistic demands are employed. Moralism only increases the pressure of crime and guilt, and never gets at or can get at the roots of the problem. DON'T SUPPRESS NATURE IN THE FIRST PLACE, THEN NO ANTISOCIAL DRIVES WILL BE CREATED AND NO COMPULSION WILL BE REQUIRED TO SUPPRESS THEM. WHAT YOU SO DESPERATELY AND VAINLY TRY TO ACHIEVE BY WAY OF COMPULSION AND ADMONITION IS THERE IN THE NEWBORN INFANT READY TO LIVE AND FUNCTION. LET IT GROW AS NATURE REQUIRES, AND CHANGE YOUR INSTITUTIONS ACCORDINGLY. We shall soon see that the trouble does not lie with the human "badness" or "sinfulness" but with the established beliefs and institutions which so persistently, over millennia, and so cruelly at times, have made it impossible to get at the naturally given morality in the human infant. Imagine a man drowning in a flood, trying to scoop the water away with a spoon instead of plugging the hole where the water is pouring from.

Now, the greatest difficulty in letting newborn infants develop their natural morality is the fact that armoring sets in so very early in life, i.e., soon after birth; thus until a short while ago scarcely anything was known about the life expressions of the infant. *With the first armor blockings the infant's self-regulatory powers begin to wane.* They become steadily weaker as the armoring spreads over the whole organism, and they *must* be replaced by compulsive, moral principles if the child is to exist and survive in its given environment. Thus, the compulsive regulation of infants is not the result of bad intentions or maliciousness on the part of educators or parents. It is an awful necessity, an emergency measure. We shall soon see how human malice enters the arena of education when the natural core functions are given full freedom. However, the basic difficulty is the actual necessity of the compulsive measures once the baby's self-regulatory core functions have been smothered by the segmentally arranged rings of armor which develop over the length of the body.* This sounds like advocating the deeds of the devil. However, unless we fully grasp the rationality in the present methods of infant upbringing, we shall never be able to replace these incompetent measures with better ones. Nobody would fight an enemy without knowing his real strength. The strength of compulsive training is the rationality, which increases with the armoring, of *having* to suppress perverted, secondary drives. Self-regulation cannot function in this realm. It is only operable in its own domain, that of the naturally given primary needs. In other words, *"self-regulation" cannot be conceived of as something to be implanted in the child, or something that can be taught. It can only grow of its own accord.* What the educator and the parents can do is protect this naturally developing self-regulation from birth onward. Since every bit of chronic armoring only weakens the functioning of self-regulation and makes compulsive training necessary, the adults' main objective is the continuous and careful removal of every type of armoring that may appear in the infant. This requires:

*See *Character Analysis,* Chapter XIV, "The Expressive Language of the Living."

1. Thorough knowledge of what armoring is and how it functions.

2. Training in observing and handling the first appearances of armoring.

3. Avoidance of any mixing of concepts. One cannot mix a bit of self-regulation with a bit of moral demand. Either we trust nature as basically decent and self-regulatory or we do not, and then there is only one way, that of training by compulsion. It is essential to grasp the fact that the two ways of upbringing do not go together. The child will only get confused and disjointed in its emotional structure if both moral compulsion and self-regulation are employed. Worst of all, of course, is self-regulatory training by compulsive demand.

DIFFICULTIES IN
GENITAL DEVELOPMENT

It is to be hoped that by the time our children are grown, the emotional plague will be curbed in its rampant, gossipy malignancy to a sufficient degree that what is reported here about their genital development will not be misused to smear them and to defile their character. It would appear quite impossible to work out the problems of healthy children if we were to shrink from utterly frank discussion of their intimate experiences.

David's genital trouble began when, at about three, the cover of a toilet seat fell on the tip of his penis as he was urinating. He bled a little and cried bitterly. But he soon overcame the shock. Accidents like this would remain harmless, without lasting effect, if the emotional experiences which are so easily anchored in such trauma did not occur. During the summer of that same year, his parents took a mother with a little girl about the same age as David into the house. The woman was to do the housekeeping. David made friends easily, and he attached himself to the little girl. She was already slightly armored and had developed a certain degree of hypocrisy. But healthy aliveness shone through these still-superficial distortions, and the two children had a very good time together. They began to play intimate games, which tended toward full genital activity. One day David appeared very disturbed. He was annoyed by little, unimportant things, was cranky, and obnoxious in a quite unusual manner; in brief, he was neurotic. His parents did not understand what had happened. The emotional disturbance did not diminish. On the contrary, it grew in intensity to such an extent that the whole self-regulatory regime seemed to be in jeopardy.

At this point an extremely important, hitherto unknown fact emerged clearly: *Neurotic behavior cannot be dealt with by means of self-regulation. It forces authoritarian measures.* This close interrelation between biopathic behavior and authoritarian countermeasures seems to be automatic. Self-regulation appears to have no place in and no influence upon emotions which do not come from the living core directly but only as if through a thick hard wall. Moreover, one has the impression that secondary drives cannot stand self-regulatory conditions of existence. They force sharp discipline on the part of the educator or parent. It is as if a child with an essentially secondary-drive structure feels that it cannot function or exist without disciplinary guidance. This is paralleled by the interlacing of self-regulation in the healthy child with self-regulation in the environment. Here the child cannot function unless it has freedom of decision and movement. It cannot tolerate discipline any more than the armored child can tolerate freedom.

These insights are new, unheard of, difficult to grasp clearly right away. They need extensive study and discussion. However, they are in agreement with the basic functional identity of organism and environment and their mutual interdependence. The disciplinary environment rests on the suppression of the natural, primary, self-regulatory emotions, and the thwarted emotional structure responds in agreement with the disciplinary environment, supporting and reproducing it. Self-regulation, freedom of movement and decision seem to find no place in this setup.

On the other hand, self-regulatory conditions rely on the natural emotional reactions, are fed by them and strengthened by natural self-regulation in the individual. Here the disciplinary procedure is foreign, and out of place.

We are dealing with two entirely different kinds of existence which do not mix. If a self-regulatory child is transplanted suddenly into a disciplinary environment, it will become disoriented and eventually sick. If a child brought up in a disciplinary manner is transplanted into a self-regulatory environment, it too will at first lose its balance and be less well adapted than in the usual authoritarian environment.

David had come in touch with disciplinary, authoritarian life conditions when he became attached to the little girl. He began to do things he had never done before. And his parents felt utterly helpless, to such an extent that they too, though highly conscious of self-regulation, felt like sliding into the other way of life—by necessity.

The mother of the girl was a little woman who had been abandoned by her husband. She was little in body and little in spirit. She had tried hard to make the best of what she knew about bringing up a child; "the best" in this case being to please the neighbors and disregard the child as much as possible. She admonished and nagged the girl to

do this or that, or to stop doing this or that, all day long,
especially in the presence of David's parents. She obviously
tried to please. She had had to fight hard for her existence,
and showing off a "well-behaved" child seemed a part of
her means of earning a living. She was of German origin.
The disciplinary tone was accordingly continuous. The
child had been beaten a lot by both father and mother.
Still, she had retained some of her original natural charm.
She quite clearly hated her mother and made fun of her
behind her back. She already had restricted respiration
and an initial rigidity of the body. Within a few weeks the
child had grasped the atmosphere of freedom in David's
home. Withdrawn at first, she slowly emerged from her
hiding and began to flourish. Now one could see clearly
that the mother, though enjoying this change, simultaneously disliked it intensely. She feared that her child
would have difficulties in going back to the strict, ascetic
environment in which she usually lived.

People living in reduced circumstances usually develop
a much stricter regime with children than people in better
conditions. The daily struggle for existence, the restricted
finances, the fear of public opinion, the physical closeness
of the family members, and other similar factors tend to
create a very unwholesome situation for children. Most
rebels against established social mores and institutions
stem from such homes, in which they have lived stringently
and under strict authoritarian discipline. Rebellion is structuralized early in life, and is later turned against anything
and everything, regardless of whether or not it is worth
preserving. The emphasis is on rebellion and not on the
goal of social change. It is envy of better living conditions
much more than rational rebellion for better homes for all
which is at the root of such character molding. Eastern,
patriarchal Jewish homes, with their strict early religious

training, their resignation from all joy in life, their feeling
of being ostracized, are breeding places for such irrational
rebellion and cruelty in getting at the "rich." It has little
to do with the rational aim of restricting vile exploitation
of workers. Proof of this is seen easily in the fact that not
a single political revolution has ever improved the lot of
people at large. Rebels who later become leaders of mass
movements are more cruel, more authoritarian, more prone
to exploit human helplessness than anyone they have
fought ever was. Remember the little rebel Hitler. Also,
understand the connection of Stalin's early seminary education and the asceticism in the later Bolshevist ideology.

What appears to be most marked are the contradictions
in sexual living. On the one hand, pornography and de-
basement of sexual relations are rampant in restricted,
little homes; on the other hand, the children of such homes
tend, if they do not emerge as gangsters of one kind or
another, to react sharply against the sexual smut which
they experienced early in life. They seem to be ashamed,
embarrassed about this background when facing the moral
superstructure of society, and they usually suppress sexual
manifestations much more cruelly than do others.

In the early days of the Russian Revolution prostitution
was fought as a social evil; the prostitute was not guilty.
Later on, *all* sexual expression was fought; the marital laws
became stricter than in any other country, children's sexuality was regarded as evil, and wherever the Communists
marched in, they put "to work" girls who were entertainers
in bars and similar places. The punishment entailed in these
measures had nothing whatsoever to do with fighting exploitation of the female body; otherwise, they would have
understood that there was some basic human need,
thwarted as it was, behind such social institutions as
brothels and teahouses.

This general review of the background of little people's feelings will better illuminate what happened to David. He had begun playing genitally with the girl. They embraced and kissed each other quite in the open, and they often went to bed together. David told his parents later that one day they had been caught naked together by the girl's mother. The girl got a severe beating and David was told that she would drown him in the lake. He did not immediately report this incident to his parents, which is a problem in itself. We shall see later how powerful the influence of the emotional plague is, and how much faster it is absorbed than that of rational conduct.

For the first time, David had met the emotional plague. It was a very bad experience. The mother was dismissed, and she and her little girl left, but David remained cranky. He was clearly under severe nervous strain. He was frequently spiteful and often held his breath when he cried. At that time little was known about the use of orgone therapy with small children.

David's genitality appeared to have vanished. He developed a mild phobia that wolves would appear in his room. But this phobia soon subsided. His father approached the problem first by simple, casual talks. He told his son to come to him when he felt troubled. Thereafter the boy reestablished his "talks with father," revealing a story which renders all high-sounding treatises on education perfectly useless.

David hooked on immediately to talks they had had previously when the child was about two years old. Then he had wondered why his mother had hair at her genitals. Now he thought that a wolf might be hidden in her body; that the hair belonged to the head of the wolf. Here it became evident that genital anxiety was making its appearance for the first time: *he must not approach the female genital*. The punishment the little girl received from her mother for partaking in genital play confirmed the danger. Another little girl with whom he had developed an intimate relationship had, so he told his father quite spontaneously, refused to let him play with her genitals. The pain he had experienced in his penis when the cover of the toilet had fallen down was another reminder of danger. In brief, David was in genital trouble, and there seemed to be no way to get at it. Talking alone was of little use. True, it took away some of his worries; he had somebody to come to when in trouble. But the basic genital block did not budge. He passed through his fifth and sixth years with no genital interests, not even self-satisfaction.

A few months after the mother and her little girl had gone, David developed a pathological interest in matches. He asked to light matches again and again. His father sensed the pathological nature of this behavior but did not know what to do about it. To forbid it would surely have caused the child to lie and conceal his playing with matches, but to allow it would further a pathological trait. It was decided to tell David that he could light a match whenever his father or mother smoked a cigarette. In doing so, he showed more than a simple interest in lighting a match. He seemed to become strangely excited. The father gradually tried to find out what he felt when he lit a match. David told him frankly that he felt "peculiar" in his eyes and in his belly. Here it became clear that the action of lighting a match somehow excited his autonomic nervous system. Several weeks passed by, and David would strike matches whenever a cigarette was lit. He was explicitly told not to light any matches when he was alone and to be aware of the danger of fire. He seemed to understand and to agree. One day, however, the biopathic nature of the activity was revealed clearly.

Early one morning David's parents saw smoke coming out from around the door of his room. They rushed into the room and found several burned-out matches under the bed, as well as some rags which had caught fire and were smoldering. His parents felt that the situation was out of hand. David had not reacted in his usual way. Obviously he had developed a typical arson compulsion. They felt helpless, did not know what to do. The child seemed to expect punishment, a beating or something of that sort. His father did not touch him but told him very strictly that if this kind of thing happened again he would have to send him away from their home. Now this was quite definitely a mistake, even though it was in conformity with usual practice. It was an expression of helplessness, as is always the case in such situations. I dare to generalize that *all disciplinary measures are due to helplessness and ignorance of how to proceed rationally.*

David's behavior began to become biopathic. He was nasty and cranky more often. Such behavior cannot be mastered with a few gymnastic tricks, nor can it be helped with massage, intelligence tests, discipline, love alone, although love soothes the trouble. It must first be well *understood.* David's father knew that the crankiness was somehow the result of feelings of distress in the body. The blocking in the throat was a major cause of the trouble, but it could not account for the chronic distress since it appeared only sporadically with crying or acute anger. Something else was the responsible factor.

In retrospect, it is hard to explain why David's father did not approach the child orgone-therapeutically. Until 1947, no medical attempts to get at children's biopathies had been made. There had been a few experiments but they lacked a strict scientific basis and thus yielded no techniques that could be applied practically. It should be emphasized repeatedly that "letting out emotions" or "breaking a block" here or there is not useful because it does not represent a well-reasoned, scientific approach. Any sensitive person engaged in gymnastics can alleviate acute discomfort, but he does not know what he is doing nor why he is doing it. He could not teach it or apply it as a therapeutic system. This does not imply that such help is of no value. It only means that no basic, socially valid procedures can be built on it, either in curing or in preventing disease.

Thus, there was nothing to do but to observe carefully and start helping when a first thorough understanding was reached.

A few weeks after the fire incident, David developed a slight stutter. This came as a terrible shock. David had always spoken well, so well that his parents had begun to see him as a future writer or performer. Now he began to stutter. The father was well aware that stuttering is a most insidious symptom, hard to get rid of once it is acquired. It is a chronic and humiliating ailment. In addition, the father's pride was deeply hurt. His son, whose self-regulatory development had given him such satisfaction and whom he had expected to be a model for children of the future, was now a stutterer. Nothing worse could have happened.

These details are brought forth at some length with a certain purpose in mind. It will be shown that there is little more detrimental to the cause of healthy functioning in children than child therapists who are strutting around boasting about what they can accomplish in a few sessions with a few manipulations; or parents who react to misery in their children with hurt pride, fearing what public opinion will say about them. It is quite natural that one's pride is hurt or that one feels utter defeat. It would be unnatural if the parents' pride was not hurt and if they did not worry about the social consequences of such mishaps.

What is essential, however, is whether such feelings are immediately recognized and kept in check. It is far better for all concerned to *feel* such reactions and to curb them than to harbor them unconsciously, and from then onward to develop all kinds of irrational, ugly, harmful attitudes toward the child which only help the disease symptom to become permanent.

How harmful the consequences of false pride are should be a subject of deep reflection. The parent who knows that his pride is hurt will do less harm than the one who is hurt but is too proud to admit it. In general, emotions in the open, no matter of what kind, are far preferable to emotions that remain hidden. The latter will inevitably turn into chronic falsehood, once described by an experienced educator as "greenish-yellowish-shallow-muddy staleness." There are few things more damaging to a child than the chronic, smooth, eternally kindly, "never-raise-the-voice" attitude of so many so-called modern educators, who condemn any expression of healthy aggression in the child. They do not distinguish between natural aggressiveness, which is good and healthy; destructiveness, which can be natural; and sadism, which is always biopathic.

To return to David: When he began to stutter, his father told me he felt utter despair and a sense of complete failure. Therefore, he did not try to interfere right away. He let enough time pass to curb these natural but harmful reactions. Then he talked to the boy. He told him not to worry about the difficulty he had in uttering some syllables; it would disappear again. Furthermore, he asked David to tell him exactly what he had felt when his father had reprimanded him severely for having struck matches in such a dangerous way. David told him that he had felt like *biting his father's nose off*.

This was the first, very important access to the stuttering.

David had obviously blocked off severe hatred in his jaw. Stammering and stuttering are direct expressions of armored jaw and throat muscles. The oral, anal, and other elements which are found analytically in stuttering are secondary additions, fill-ins, as it were. The mechanism proper is contraction in the mouth and throat muscles which cannot be overcome by the movements involved in the formulation of certain syllables. Later on, once the stuttering is established, shame, feelings of inferiority, and apprehension are added and aggravate the symptom, making it chronic. But the core is a simple acute armoring of the muscle group which is used in speech. Thus, the core of stammering and stuttering is of a *physiological*, bioenergetic nature; it has been brought about by an emotional upheaval and is maintained by emotional complications.

It was at this point that David's father began his "first aid." He advised everyone in the household not to pay any attention to David's trouble. Then he explained to the child that he must get out the hate he had felt in the match incident. He let him contract his jaw muscles; then he told him to "yap" at his father as if wanting to bite him. David could not do it right away, but within a few days he not only could do it perfectly but he enjoyed it very much. When this was accomplished, his father let him kick him and hit him with his fists. David loved it. He let go fully. He began boxing. He was now a sheriff who knocked out bad men. Furthermore, his father told him that he could light matches in his presence whenever he smoked a cigarette. David was clearly relieved of some severe pressure when he could light matches again. From then on, he would light a match whenever it was needed in the household.

Slowly his father began again to inquire about the kind and location of the feeling and sensations the boy had when lighting matches. David then told him that he felt "tickling in his eyes." This was new and incomprehensible to his father. The following assumption could be made, however. David's eyes would become dull when he was in a cranky mood. This dullness apparently felt strange and bothersome to him, since his self-perception usually included sparkling and lively eyes. Lighting matches thus probably constituted an irritation of the optical nerves, restoring some of his accustomed feeling of liveliness in the eyes. Lighting matches, and maybe all forms of arson compulsion, could well be understood as attempts to reinstate a higher level of excitation in the organism.

Further observation revealed that the "getting stuck in the throat" was accompanied more and more by severe rigidity in the diaphragmatic segment. It became necessary to relieve the blocks in the throat and diaphragm whenever they appeared, right away and thoroughly. This should prevent these blocks from establishing themselves as chronic structural constituents of a total armoring.

It appears necessary now to pause and consider the wider social implications of these procedures: We must assume that bringing up healthy children will not be simple and easy, even when the basic functions of health are fully known. As I said before, sick functioning at present still crowds out healthy functioning, and will again and again interfere with our children's development. This may go on for decades, if not for centuries to come, should there be social conditions like wars, economic depressions, etc. It is not necessarily the conclusion of a pessimistic or disillusioned mind to assume that the mass of armored and mechanistically oriented human animals will again and again kill life in one way or another. They will again and again shrink from full recognition of the requirements of the living. Militarism, politics, greedy business practices will continue to set expediency, power, and profit before the interest of the child. It is, therefore, only reasonable to prepare well in advance for the events which will inevitably turn up as attempts to hamper the establishment of naturally functioning human character structures. These events will be mostly of a structural nature, i.e., not due to any evil, conscious intent. Nobody will really be able or willing to fight openly against the healthy child of the future. It will be done quite "innocently" by severely armored *homines normales* who will find a million excuses why children in their first puberty should not be free to play genital games; why self-regulation should be restricted here and there in the "interest of the state," of "national security," or "religious feeling," or "in order not to hurt anybody's feelings unnecessarily"; why "cultural interests" and "social obligations" should be considered "too." In the maze of crowded events and tasks to be fulfilled, there will probably be little time to penetrate the dense fog thus created again and again by the haters of childhood and happiness. The basic task of securing healthy functioning in children will be slowed down or even completely jeopardized. Children growing up in these years will feel the impact of the struggle between conflicting social influences—on the one hand, the free movement of self-regulatory forces and, on the other, the compulsive force of armored public opinion. Many children will fall victim to the emotional plague, as they have for thousands of years. It will be all the more dangerous because the emotional plague will not proceed directly and openly against the healthy child but will disguise its hate in many devious ways. Children growing up in this period of transition, no matter how long it lasts, will need the support of exact knowledge about the first signs of armoring. This knowledge will never be complete; it will never be able to cope fully with the critical situations as they arise. But it will rely on the general feeling for the laws of life on the part of millions of people who have this knowledge in their "guts." They will be the simple people, people close to nature or work or accomplishment. Thus, most probably, the educational and medical centers which will be responsible for the Children of the Future will be in touch with and will enjoy the support of these growing islands of knowledge about nature and health. However, this knowledge will not help them unless they succeed practically in overcoming the armoring whenever it appears in each new generation, and in preventing it from taking root in the children's organisms. Then, and only then, is there reliable hope that these children will in turn provide new generations of educators and physicians who will do the same job with their children, but still better, safer, and with more support from a growing public opinion in their favor.

It is this anticipation of the future that rendered the detailed work on David so important. Every bit of experience with incipient armoring and the means to prevent it from becoming chronic was of far greater importance at this time than bringing up a "completely healthy child." If it was possible to keep a child fairly healthy even under adverse outer conditions, then there would be hope for the Children of the Future.

I used to teach the physicians who studied with me that to know and handle one's limitations and mistakes was always of much greater value for the final outcome of the task than to have a quick, neat result and then sit back. The quick, one-day celebrities who can impress the multitude with their fine accomplishments, without ever worrying about the obstacles in the way of the task ahead or the emotional plague, which has so destructively obfuscated for millennia every human attempt at betterment of the situation, must be severely criticized and checked. They are dangerous, because they blind us to the obstacles in the way. They are personally and ambitiously involved in their successes and, not being well-rooted in accomplishment, they grow like weeds. The credulous crowd follows them blindly, without thinking, and without seeing things as they are. These "brilliant" performers on the public stage are like comets which rise rapidly in the sky and just as rapidly fall into oblivion. What they leave is a big mess to be cleaned up by the slow, hardworking moles in their daily, patient, modest, persistent, and faithful efforts.

The simultaneous release of the acute blocking in David's jaw and diaphragm, the repeated outbursts of rage, and the toleration of lighting matches had drawn off enough energy from the symptomatic stuttering. Three weeks after it first appeared, it disappeared. During the following few months, very occasionally a syllable did not come out quite right. David's parents joked about it, repeated the stumbling in a playful manner, and then the last traces of this otherwise dangerously chronic habit vanished. David's clear speech returned fully.

The whole episode had been quite a lesson; it also convinced us that without a chronic biopathic background there is no soil for the rooting of neurotic symptoms. This was a major gain in knowledge. The question now was whether and how it would be possible to prevent chronic armoring in David during the next two to three years. One could assume that once the first puberty had been passed through without armoring, there would be no major trouble ahead until the second puberty.

There was not yet any sign of genitality, although it was overdue; David was already in his sixth year. There was no masturbation and no genital approach to girls of his age; also, no genital interest and no erections. This was a great worry to David's parents. His pelvis did not move quite as freely as the rest of his body. It was not stiff in the full meaning of the word, but its motility was somewhat restricted. When he ran, for instance, his pelvis would not completely follow the swings of his body; it would be dragged along slightly. Upon examination, I found that his pelvis could be moved passively, indicating that no spastic contractions had as yet set in. But when told to move his pelvis actively, the child could not do it and moved his whole torso instead. David's father decided to mobilize the pelvis, since its restricted motility seemed to be the basis for the lack of genitality. We can clearly see how very far education has traveled over the past ten to twenty years. Before, fathers used to beat or admonish their sons for playing with their genitals. Now David's father was desperate because genital play had *not* developed. In this complete turnabout of attitude the core of the "sexual revolution" is well expressed. The attitude has shifted from sex negative to sex positive. In between lies the vast domain of the present-day, noncommittal position of "Don't touch it" on the part of the majority of modern educators. They still "divert" children from genital games; they still refuse to talk about sex freely, or they talk about it too late, or in terms of "how to tell it to the boy." It is essential to note how different this is from the orgonomic standpoint.

Orgonomy takes notice of bioenergetic blocking and armoring in the child. It tries to establish measures to prevent chronic armoring. It helps the child in its conflicts with a world of armored human beings. It tells the child that people who beat children for playing doctor or father and mother are ignorant and mistaken.

The rest of the story can be brief:

During the winter of 1949–50, David's parents moved to another city and he went to a new school. He became ill.

He was pale, anemic, had a fast heartbeat, fainted several times in school when working to keep up with the children in his class, who were about a year older than he. Once he collapsed and was brought home in a state of exhaustion. He recovered soon, but remained anemic and continued to have a rapid heartbeat. He chose to drop back a grade and returned to kindergarten. At this time, his father reported that he felt the child was headed toward "rheumatic fever." It is much too early to say anything final about the possible connection between so-called rheumatic fever and a bio-energetic lag in the lower part of the organism. It seems plausible that if the bioenergetic functioning in the pelvis is not fully developed, the bioenergy seizes the upper part of the body and thus affects the heart. It would be impossible as yet to establish exactly how this connection comes about. But the medical orgonomist has good reason to assume that such childhood diseases as rheumatic fever, etc., have some intimate relationship to the malfunctioning of infantile genitality. This chapter of medicine has not yet been opened, but it will be soon. A few such cases that I have seen and scrutinized from the standpoint of the bio-energetic background indicate the correctness of the above assumption. David's father was convinced that the boy was in danger of acquiring a chronic heart ailment, and he said so at the clinical demonstration. With my help, he kept fighting for a soft body in David. This fight met with success a few months later.

David befriended another little girl his age, and an intense love relationship developed. The parents of the girl were sympathetic and things developed well. David began to recover.

He still used to go to his father for a "talk" or a "session," but much less frequently. The ruddy color in his cheeks returned. His blood was normal again. The rapidity of his heartbeat subsided. His parents report that now, six months later, David is emotionally in full swing in every respect. He has a genital love relationship with a little girl; his diaphragm and pelvis are mobile; there has been no recurrence of the stuttering; he is not tired or morose or inclined to become neurotically cranky. He is passing through his first puberty without further trouble. Whether or not the trouble he has had will affect his second puberty is uncertain. But as long as he has skilled first aid ready to assist him when he "gets stuck," there is little to worry about. To repeat:

We should not strive to bring up children who have no trouble at all, but children who are free of pathogenic armoring, so that no symptom can take root and persist. Children will get badly entangled emotionally for a long time to come. The main thing is to keep them fit enough for speedy disentanglement.

This may sound like an easy job. It is not. It will not be easy to keep our children capable of disentangling themselves from biopathic situations. The difficulty lies not with the children but with the grownups—parents, teachers, people in the environment. It depends on whether or not, and how speedily, insight into the malignancy of armoring penetrates the public at large. This, in turn, depends on how well the measures of first aid to children are developed and come into general use. It was emphasized at that first child demonstration that application of such first aid should rest primarily with parents and kindergarten teachers and not with physicians who do not take part in the child's daily life.

We shall now turn to the discussion of this new problem.

Orgonomic First Aid
for Children

When I called the first meeting of the OIRC, I had already had some valuable experiences in giving orgonomic first aid to children who had become blocked and were on the road to chronic armoring. It would be easy to collect all the many minute techniques employed in breaking the armor blocks as they appeared. However, this would not serve our purpose, which is to obtain an overview, a red thread through the maze of living reactions in an infant or child. It should be stressed most emphatically that *techniques which do not rest on a theoretical comprehension of why they are applied have no lasting value*. They are not teachable, nobody can repeat them. The procedures are haphazard, subject to the whims and personal inclinations of the particular child therapist. The ideal is a teachable and repeatable technique of orgonomic first aid which can be applied as safely as the handling of a broken rib. Of course the growing emotional structure of a child is infinitely more complicated than a bone or a machine. Nevertheless, the need for a theoretically based technique in handling emotional stress in infants is crucial. It cannot be left to the personal whim of a child therapist to decide whether or not genitality is a bioenergetic center of infantile development. Psychiatry with its psychology has suffered precisely because it places value on mere "opinions," and there is no objective control of the correctness of an opinion. We would like to see educational first aid developed in the manner of a routine experiment in science or logical deduction.* There can be no doubt that nursery school teachers or educators who have genital anxiety will not be able to handle a single phase in the emotional problems of infants. The structure of the one who is to render first aid is therefore very important. If he is emotionally blocked himself, he will be prone to develop all kinds of cockeyed ideas about what a child should be like or what to do in the event of emotional blocking. He will inevitably tend to run away from the issue at hand. The greater his personal anxieties, the farther away his judgment and practice will be from the requirements of the situation. It should be pointed out again that it is not the trouble in the child but the emotional blocking and anxieties in the educator which constitute the real difficulty. Therefore, a healthy, sexually experienced, motherly peasant woman will very often be able to find the right answer to an acute situation in a child much faster and more effectively than the most educated educator.

In dealing with children until about the fourth year of life we should remember that we are not dealing with chronic armorings where the emotions have already been obliterated, as in adult biopaths. We are handling very plastic emotional situations, initial phases of armoring, and a still free-flowing energy. There are many children whose emotional flow has been stopped right at the beginning,

---

* For example, we compress a limb that bleeds from an injury differently in the case of venous or arterial bleeding. Our operation is based on logical deduction. The same principle must be applied in educational first aid. The difference between surgical and educational first aid lies in the emotional entanglements in education. Intuition based on an essentially rational character structure will, however, always play a far greater role in education than in surgery. The lively, full contact between mother and child is and will remain irreplaceable.

who are already emotionally "dead" soon after birth. These children constitute a special problem to which access is still to be sought. We do not even know what percentage of children are emotionally deadened soon after birth, or how many retain their inborn agility through their first puberty. We do know that noisiness and biopathic hypermotility are often mistaken for natural behavior. One of the major tasks of the OIRC would be to study these questions and to reach objective criteria for what is inborn, naturally given emotional reaction and what is secondary development, due to warping of the original bioenergetic structure of the newborn infant.

Since infants are not totally armored, the technique of orgonomic character analysis as applied in biopathic grown-ups is not applicable. We cannot systematically peel off layer after layer with the goal of reaching the genital area and mobilizing genital bioenergy. In the child, before the age of four or five, genitality has not yet fully developed. The task here plainly consists of removing the obstacles in the way of natural development toward full genitality. To fulfill this task, we must agree that a first puberty in children exists; that genital games are the peak of its development; that lack of genital activity is a sign of sickness and not of health, as previously assumed; and that healthy children play genital games of all kinds, which should be encouraged and not hindered. In other words, the educator who wishes to render first aid must have a workable, logical base of operation from which he can judge and handle a given emergency situation. Yet in no other realm of human endeavor has wild, baseless, irrationally imbued opining been as rampant as in this most crucial realm of human life, i.e., the raising of children.

Fiddling around with "blocks" and "spasms" in a sick infant won't do and might even inflict more harm than good.

We must beware of the vain "healer" and "miracle worker" in child therapy, no less than of the spineless opportunist who is more interested in pleasing everybody and getting immediate mention in some pediatric or daily newspaper than he is in the child's true nature and welfare. There must be a principle in child-rearing that is in accord with the child's inborn nature. This principle must be faithfully adhered to, no matter what "culture," the local priest, or an utterly ignorant secretary of the Communist Party thinks about it. It should be clearly understood and established as a practical guideline that in dealing with children we are confronted with truly cosmic events the scope of which far exceeds the concerns of a local church or a political boss. Whoever is socially or structurally incapable of maintaining this viewpoint should not even try to approach children; he should withdraw and not disturb this important work. Every worker in this field should know that in handling children orgonomically we are participating in the most radical revolution in human life that has ever been attempted or dreamed of. We are working at the very roots of what are probably the most evil and involved contradictions of human nature. We must trust our babies' roots in nature and rely on them for the future of culture and civilization. Nobody is forced to do this job, but anyone who starts it must know what he is dealing with. No tactics, diplomacy, strategy, politics, maneuvers, compromises, evasions of the issue are applicable in this work. Nothing but the child and its life interests count. They alone will provide the answer to the mess.

The realm in which interest in the Children of the Future must operate is vast. In the newborn infant cosmic, lawful functions are given over to the social institutions of man. Everything then depends on whether these institutions are in agreement with the cosmic orgonomic laws or whether they oppose these laws and functions, i.e., whether man-made law agrees with natural law in the basic functions of life. The cosmic functioning of which the newborn infant is a sample—unspoiled, plastic, productive, free in the truest sense of the word in terms of future developments—is a vast realm beyond present-day human grasp. In the new-born, the human animal, like all other animals, is entrusted with a bit of this cosmic functioning, for which he is forever longing in his philosophies and religions. Every unthwarted mother knows this perfectly well, even if only intuitively. Her response is represented in the form of bioenergetic functioning, and is not primarily of a social origin. On the contrary, it *constitutes* social relationships. The mother's care of the newborn in any animal species is clear proof of the bioenergetic nature of breeding. Social reactions emerge later from this soil, if they can do so without interference by thwarted life. Caring for the newborn infant needs naturally rooted skills, which cannot be replaced in any way by artificial, cultural measures. The compulsion-neurotic method of feeding children on schedule, invented by Pirquet in Vienna, was devastatingly wrong and harmful to countless children. So was the binding of the limbs against natural movement. The tortures thus inflicted were unimaginable. The sadistic habit of circumcision will soon be recognized as the senseless, fanatical cruelty it truly is. We shall return to these specifically human measures when we discuss the hatred of life. At this point we are dealing with a different problem altogether. The riddle to be solved if our work for the Children of the Future is to succeed is not only, and not even primarily, what kind of evil things are being perpetrated in the rearing of infants. The riddle to be solved is: *How can the world of adults who are deal-ing with newborn infants be made aware of what is really done to unspoiled life in each new generation?*

Good things, life-important things, about infant care have been told and written and spoken of for millennia by countless people. They did not penetrate, did not form an unimpeachable public rule. Everyone has seen how animal pups grow and are cared for. Countless poems have been written about it. Yet nothing of it has penetrated into human life. Nearly every mother knows deep down what a child is and what it needs. Yet most mothers follow the hollow, harmful theories of passer-by theorists and not their own natural instincts. Thus, the trouble is not with the problems an infant presents but with something very powerful in man's character structure which is in the way of anyone who attempts to solve these problems. *It is logical, therefore, that the obstacles in the way of rational infant care are of far greater importance than the problems of the infant as such.*

Where is the entrance to the hidden ground on which parents, educators, physicians, nurses can freely receive and accept what they know deep down to be true? To the one who understands human affairs it is quite obvious that the entrance to this domain is not only hidden as are other riddles of nature; it is well guarded against entry. One thinks of the archangel who, with flaming sword, forbiddingly guards the entrance to paradise in the biblical legend of Adam and Eve. Myths have a very deep significance. The expelling of Adam and Eve from the Garden of Eden refers to man's loss of his contact with nature long ago. He cannot enter again as long as he is "sinful." From our viewpoint, he cannot return to nature because of something that contradicts nature. Since man is a tiny part of nature, he must obey its laws, lest he lose his true nature, become unfit, and land in the mess he is in now. There is not much use in calling man "back to God" unless it is finally understood what "God" actually means. Not to know

God is a part of guarding the entrance, the punishment, a part of man's downfall.

Thus, the obstacles in the way of our children growing up as God and nature have created them are great. They must be frightful if for millennia man has tried to return to himself, called it "paradise" or "liberty" or whatever you please, and again and again has failed to find the way. Somebody is guarding the entrance, something in "human nature" makes it inaccessible. And this is the reason why all fruitful human experience remains unutilized, why all great teachings of lonely voices in the wilderness meet only deaf ears or evil hatred.

It is, therefore, not the repeated description of the misery, not the admonition to do better and be better, not programs, platforms, propaganda, not idealization of the child that will ever do it. We must find the entrance to the place where the solution of the riddle has remained hidden for so long a time. We must find it, or our new effort will fail, as did so many other brave and honest efforts to get at the evil. It does not matter whether we find it today, to-morrow, or in two hundred years. It does not matter whether our first approach to the entrance fails. What matters is the direction given: *Stop trying to proclaim good advice until the entrance to the hideout of the terrible obstacle is found and mastered.*

I did not dare hope that the way in which this entrance is hidden would show up quickly or easily. Neither did I expect that the participants in the task would even understand what I was talking about. I waited patiently for the appearance of the first hurdle. Six weeks later it was there as expected, right in the midst of the OIRC. Nothing better could have happened.

Meeting the Emotional Plague

I was prepared to meet the obstacle in the way of healthy children, though I did not know when and in what form it would make its appearance in this particular setting. I had entered the project with certain secure knowledge about the nature of the emotional plague. It centered on the following facts:

1. The emotional plague is not an expression of conscious ill will or designed brutality; the *structural* character of the plague makes its effects all the more dangerous. Emotional plague is a character trait like cleanliness or diligence or truthfulness. It is biopathic behavior acted out in inter-human relationships.

2. The energy source of emotional plague reactions is basically sexual frustration combined with keen aggressiveness.

3. People afflicted with emotional plague act with the subjectively firm convictions that they are serving some good purpose. The burning of witches in the Middle Ages; the gassing of Jews in Hitler's Europe in the twentieth century; the shooting and hanging of political adversaries by the red fascists; the persecution of Negroes in the South of the United States; the killing of widows in old India; putting adolescents into reform school because they have engaged in sexual intercourse; the conviction of innocent people by overzealous district attorneys; framing an honest

man who is deemed dangerous to some interests; punishing children severely for playing genital games; attacking some country under the pretense that it is going to attack you; accusing the United States of attacking North Korea, when actually Russia invaded South Korea; smearing a rich giver when he stops giving; squeezing money from a man who divorces his wife; malignant gossip in general; defamation of character—all such human actions are performed with the deep conviction of serving a good cause. The disguise is not conscious but well rationalized.

4. All human plague reactions are basically directed against natural expressions of life. It is the spontaneously moving, the soft yielding in life expressions which provokes hate and destruction in the armored human animal.

5. People afflicted with and acting on the basis of emotional plague are generally highly gifted. Their talents, however, did not mature slowly, e.g., in diligent works of art or science or technology. They are abortive talents, quick to take advantage of the numerous situations in society which provide the greatest superficial, economic, or political success with the least effort. Thus, it is the emotionally flat man or woman with strong impulses to act who supplies the vast army of the followers and leaders of irrational movements and social groups in our society. The maliciousness of abortive geniuses like Hitler or Stalin develop from such characters.

6. It is precisely the bioenergetically strong person and not the weakling who will most likely degenerate into the ways of pestilent behavior. The condition underlying this lapse into evil is a sharp sense of life with an equally strong blocking of life expressions. This specific combination is at the basis of any and every emotional plague reaction.

7. The attraction exerted on helpless or weak human structures by these strong but frustrated biopaths is much

greater than that exerted by healthy life and natural behavior. This seems to be a paradox. Why should the evil,
the superficial, the distorted expression exert so much
greater influence than the natural, the soft, and the healthy,
if the latter and not the former is the universal ideal?
Everyone who has lived and worked within the framework
of orgonomic thought has observed this nonsensicality.
Children will identify much faster and more fully with sick,
rough stuff—grimacing, using bad language, shooting, spit-
ting, etc.—than with calm, deep, simple natural behavior.
Given the choice between deep thought and a rough foot-
ball game, the man in the street will doubtless choose the
latter. The inclination to superficiality is general. And it is
the superficiality, facility, and quick metabolism of pestilent life which most attract the human animal. Now, this is
clearly not because man feels better, lives more happily or
safely when identified with the superficial and facile. His
deep secret longing is always directed toward exactly the
opposite: toward the natural, the soft, the good, the understanding; in brief, toward what is called "godlike." Yet the
plague always seems to prevail, and it has done so for many
thousands of years. In this paradox, the riddle was hidden.
It was only through a highly specialized character-analytic
disclosure that it was solved: The natural, the "godlike," the
"good" remain inaccessible *because human character is not
structured in accordance with its requirements*. It is structured in agreement with the superficial, impulsive, aimless
way of the irrational. Processes of natural living provoke
the deepest longings to such an extent that they become
unbearable, because they cannot be fulfilled. The way of
the plague provides an outlet from this dilemma. It provides an ideal to which one can become oriented *without
actually having to change one's way of life*. Thus, it is possible to remain sitting in the mess while one's soul is warmed

in the glare of high ideals, to remain a worm, crawling miserably on this earth, but to have a national honor or be a "crusader" for one thing or another.

It is one of the most tragic as well as the most peculiar irrationalisms that a man is ready to risk his life for a state ideal or a crusade of any sort, while he will cringe and be a coward when called upon to stand up for the simplest conviction about life or work or love or children or truth. This is quite obvious to everyone and need not be elaborated. The extent of this typical irrationality in man's structure can be measured by the applause and admiration bestowed on the rare individual who stands up for truth or love or life or the child. Why should the self-evident and the obvious be so rare and the irrational so rampant if not because of the inability to live truth and love and life? There is more to it, however, for from this weakness emerges hatred, all human hatred against anything that is consistent with natural living.

8. The subject of the hatred directed against the living is vast, complicated, and barely touched on. We must be satisfied merely to obtain a glimpse of its outlines. No official science, philosophy, or educational theory has, to my knowledge, ever dealt with it.

Evasion and hatred of the living principle are the two outstanding characteristics of human behavior. And the term "living" must be taken in its broadest sense. The living comprises not only its core functions, genitality and *joie de vivre*, but also such disparate life-positive functions as truth, directness, undisguised naturalness, basic creativeness, deviation from the well-trodden paths of the armored little man.

The deep, murderous hatred against anything alive is well known and has often been splendidly described by writers. The problem, as mentioned before, is not the existence of the hatred and knowledge of its functions but the complete inability of these facts to penetrate the human herd. Not a single effort to eliminate this hatred has succeeded. Therefore, the main objective in a rational, crucial attempt to come to grips with the plague must be to provide the appropriate soil in human awareness where such knowledge can grow and exert its effects against the plague.

THE KILLING OF LIFE

I knew very well that there is seldom a human structure brought up under the stress of emotional frustration in early infancy which does not contain a layer of bitter hatred against life. Just as the first roentgenologists fell victim to deadly X-ray burns because precautionary measures were unknown, so the first medical and educational orgonomists had not yet developed adequate measures to protect themselves against the bitter, murderous hatred which met them whenever they took a step forward in learning about life. Ten years before the establishment of the OIRC there was no awareness of the methods of the emotional plague. I was taken quite unaware on several occasions, not knowing what was happening. At that time I was virtually alone in my fight, with only a few friends. Now, in 1950, my work was known worldwide, and many professional and lay people were in one way or another associated with it. So I not only had to protect myself and my work, I also had to protect the workers who joined me and were quite innocent regarding the emotional plague. How could I guide them? I decided, first, to keep careful watch over their structural behavior and, second, to warn them repeatedly of the hatred against the living which had been rampant for millennia. I knew that whoever has not personally experienced emotional plague reactions would not understand or be able to believe that such malignancy exists.

The basic requirements for educational and medical workers in the realm designated "Children of the Future" were these:

1. Decisions and procedures were to be made only on the basis of work and accomplishment, not mere opinion or personal friendships.

2. Utter humility in the face of the gigantic task and, at the same time, strong self-confidence attained through personal effort and accomplishment.

3. Interest in the welfare of future generations, as compared with present-day personal or professional friendships.

4. Development of a clear, rational hate of the killer of life, no matter who or what he was. Considerate behavior toward individuals was to go hand in hand with the question of whether this considerateness hampered the welfare and happiness of innumerable newborn infants. To avoid hurting the personal feelings of one sick person when the care of a whole infant generation was involved would amount to gross irresponsibility.

5. Firmness in the pursuit of truth and sharp self-criticism in the execution of this task.

6. Restriction of the disease called "socialitis," i.e., sacrifice of basic principles to social affiliations.

7. Last but not least, always to keep two questions in mind when major decisions were to be made or situations judged: What in the given situation is FOR and what is AGAINST the principle of the living and of natural self-regulation. The first had to be encouraged; the second to be understood and, if possible, fought.

It was hoped that these basic attitudes would provide a safe ground on which to meet the expected onslaught of the emotional plague on the infant research work. To judge from my former experiences, it would be foolhardy suicide to go into the field without these structural safeguards. And, in contradistinction to any cruel dictator, I refused to risk the lives of my coworkers unnecessarily. I also knew that only practical experience in the field would convince them of the necessity of these safeguards.

THE FIRST ENCOUNTER
WITH STRUCTURAL HATE

Five meetings had been held, and five comparatively healthy, self-regulated children had been demonstrated and discussed in the OIRC. In order to widen the framework, I suggested that a mother from outside the circle be invited to discuss her child. This mother had been known for quite some time as a member of a group of people from all walks of life who had joined in discussing the principle of self-regulation in early child-rearing. The mother was neither professionally nor personally affiliated in any way with the work. It was hoped that she would open another new avenue to the problem of whether educational first aid could be entrusted to mothers and fathers, rather than to less involved physicians or educators.

The meeting was introduced with a renewed warning that what was heard had to be treated with utter confidentiality. It was stressed again that the basic procedure was oriented according to the question: What in the social and personal structure is FOR and what is AGAINST the principle of self-regulation in child-rearing?

Let us keep clearly in mind that the professional audience which listened to this mother's story was composed of highly trained and carefully chosen people. They all had been or were going through therapeutic restructuring. They had read the orgonomic literature; they had heard about and learned to recognize professionally the structural hatred against the living; they had joined in this task of fighting the emotional plague; they were, on the average, far ahead of others in understanding the importance of genital health in infants and adolescents. Until this sixth meeting, they had cooperated with and followed the proceedings splendidly. Yet, the structural hatred against the living broke out in this meeting, and only I was aware of it. I had prepared myself to meet it sooner or later, but the form in which this hatred manifested itself surprised and shocked even me. Here is a brief account of this experience. The reader should be aware of the great difficulty in recounting an emotional situation which was expressed wordlessly.

The mother was a lively, intelligent, and slightly belligerent, hardworking, self-supporting woman. She was not burdened with formal cultural restrictions. She had lived her love life according to her needs and bravely fought off the moralistic mire which had so often threatened to engulf her. She had raised her child in a way that agreed with her sense for life, rather than public opinion. Naturally, she had often been forced into a defensive position and was understandably a bit high-strung. She had always searched for understanding and approval of her way of life and her natural sense of what was truly moral and decent, so when she joined some groups of lay people who made it their job to study orgonomy and sex-economy, she felt relieved. Finally, she thought, there was a group of highly trained professional people who would understand and approve of her. She had been eager to present her child to the OIRC, not only to help in this important task, but also in the hope of ceasing to be so desperately alone in her life.

She began her presentation and answered questions in an open, utterly frank, uninhibited way. As the discussion proceeded, however, she became increasingly tense. Her voice did not flow as freely as before; she spoke as if against an obstacle. Her face was flushed.

The child, whom I had seen and examined the previous day, behaved very peculiarly. She clung to her mother; it was difficult to make contact with her. She refused to undress. I did not try to force the issue, feeling that the child should be free to choose her own way. The demonstration turned into a failure. I felt a definite coldness in the atmosphere, especially when the mother began to describe the genital habits of her child. There were very few questions from the audience. When the mother left, an icy stillness prevailed. As if to break the chilly atmosphere, one social worker said loudly, "We thank you."

The discussion began. I waited. What would happen now? This mother had been the first case to test how and if we could pursue this work with the general public. The answer was now at hand.

The discussion started as if it were pushing against some unseen but immovable obstacle. The case had presented a multitude of crucial educational as well as social problems: The typical fate of an unmarried mother; the courage to resist public opinion unaided and, sometimes, in a confused way; the success of having reared a fairly healthy, lovely girl up to the age of four; the difficulties which had evolved in the child-mother relationship due to the fact that the mother had to earn a living, the father being absent; the natural skill with which this mother, untrained and unaided, had fought off the wrong advice and admonitions of aunts and grandmothers and neighbors; the consequences to be drawn from this case about the forming of public opinion, community living, the problem of unwed mothers, and many other questions. Yet the discussion did not seem to get going. I still waited and did nothing.

Finally, the discussion began to develop. It was amazing to witness the evasion of the essential, the bypassing of the issue at hand, and its replacement by petty criticism. Some felt that too much time had been devoted to questioning the mother. Others felt that I should have asked questions in a different manner, though it was not indicated in what different manner. One physician, who otherwise always appeared composed and academic, suddenly burst out: "And these seats should be more comfortable. . . ." Another participant felt highly embarrassed about the open discussion of an "illegitimate" child in front of so many people. (She admitted this frankly after the meeting.)

The petty criticism concentrated more and more on me; I should have done this and I should have done that. The child should not have been brought in during the questioning of the mother. One participant felt that the child could have been harmed by listening to the description of her genital games. Another felt that the child had not responded as was expected.

I still waited and let the barrage of petty talk go on. It was essential to find out how far it would go.

One educator boasted that she had discussed the genitality of children before an audience of three hundred people with whom she had felt compelled to raise the issue. I shuddered. How utterly naïve and removed from any sense of danger this approach was! I knew that the educator who said this had suffered from severe genital anxiety. Someone else reproached me for not having made contact with the child. I should have handled her as skillfully as I had handled another child some weeks before. I admitted that I could not make contact with the child as I had done on the previous day; that was precisely why I had failed. I did not mention the embarrassment I had felt during the questioning period.

The situation grew more and more tense. The petty criticism came at me like machine-gun bullets.

Finally, one highly skilled educational social worker broke the ice. She said, frankly, that she had felt most uncomfortable in this group of professional people. They were stiff, made no contact with each other, were mostly cold to the burning questions, in brief, they did not fit the task.

I still waited and encouraged further ventilation of the issue.

It was perfectly clear to me that structural hatred against the public discussion of down-to-earth genitality had, for the first time, attacked the OIRC. It was important to let the reactions develop further. During the confusion that beset the meeting I felt that the task itself was faced with a severe crisis. If it was impossible to carry it through with these trained and devoted professional people, then there was no other way. The OIRC was doomed.

I announced that we would have a thorough discussion of the incident at the following meeting and merely told the gathering that for the first time they had met a major obstacle in their own structures.

A few of the physicians and educators spoke privately with me after the meeting. Some had felt the hate clearly. One admitted that the mother's frankness had made her feel most uncomfortable. It was agreed that this reaction should be brought into the open at the next meeting, at the risk of a complete breakdown of the whole project. A social worker was asked to get in touch with the mother the following day to find out whether the child had suffered any harm. All those present agreed that we had been dealing with a crucial experience and that further elaboration and clarification were of paramount importance.

I felt depressed. Had I failed irreparably? I saw no way to cope with this hatred. I did not doubt that I was dealing with structural hatred, the same type that had, for so long, kept the issue of infantile genitality out of every meeting of educators and physicians all over the world; the hate that had caused the torture of countless infants through millennia; the hate against my work.

The do-not-touch-it-or-else atmosphere, unspoken, hidden, cruel, mean, ready to defame and to break any man or woman who dared to touch the forbidden domain; the murder of Christ; the endless killing all over this planet; the silent, underhanded, bitter hatred of the core of the living. The hate that drove natural love everywhere onto the back stairs and into parked automobiles; the silent but agonizing frustrations; the bitter crying of adolescents in lonely rooms; the sadists who persecuted the truth about these matters wherever it tried to penetrate the fog; the sickly grin on the face of the pestilent slanderer who listens to talks on love; the Hitlerian or Stalinite mystic who feels like cutting throats whenever he witnesses the genital embrace; the silly giggle in movie houses when fish or birds are seen mating; the binding of infants' hands to prevent them from touching the love organ; the desperate fight of decent adolescents against the experience of love turning into filth because of frustration; the martyrdom of millions of highly gifted adolescents and young people who know the truth in a confused way, get hopelessly caught, are helpless, desperate, and go crazy, only to be tortured in cruel, monstrous mental institutions where sadists of psychiatry cut their frontal lobe or kill aliveness by means of electric shock; the many thousands of adolescent boys and girls who become gangsters because their life is being wasted and they can see no way out for their natural feelings.

All this and much more passed before my eyes during a sleepless night. Would I succeed? Or would the emotional plague prevail?

During the following week I thought the situation over again and again. The task had doubtless run into a serious crisis. The problem was not the crisis itself but the structural nature of the hostile reaction which made it inaccessible. Several reports from participants indicated that they felt disturbed. There was no outward sign of actual hostility. Everything seemed calm, but at the same time, everyone knew that something crucial had happened. I faced the task of penetrating the structural wall, well aware of the great responsibility involved. Success or failure would be decisive for generations to come.

In my quandary, I remembered a quotation from D. H. Lawrence:

I've got real bitterness in my soul, just now, as if they were traitors—they are traitors. They betray the real truth. They come to me and they make me talk, and they enjoy it, it gives them a profoundly gratifying sensation. And that is all. As if what I say were meant to only give them gratification because of the flavor of my personality, as if I were a cake or a wine or a pudding. Then they say I, D. H. Lawrence, am wonderful, I am an exceedingly valuable personality, but that the things I say are extravagances, illusions. They say I cannot think. . . . All that is dynamic in the world, they convert into a sensation, to the gratification of what is static. They are static, static, static; they come, they say to me, "You are wonderful, you are dynamic," then they filch my life for a sensation unto themselves; all my effort which is my life they betray, they are like Judas: they turn it all to their own static selves, convert it into the static nullity. The result is for them a gratifying sensation, a tickling, and for me a real bleeding.

Lawrence's complaint grasped the crux of this crisis. Having been deceived by the admiration I enjoyed for many years, I realized that what drove people to me was my "brilliance" and my "radiant personality," not the cause for which I bled in many ways. I wanted workers, fighters, knowers, searchers. What I got was a lot of mystical hangers-on who expected salvation from me, orgastic potency, happiness in life, without doing anything to get and secure it. I should *give* it to them. My most bitter enemies had always been those who were thrilled by my work and the promise it harbored for mankind, but who did not have the patience, endurance, knowledge, or spirit to live it and carry it onward. I did everything possible to eliminate the mystical admirer, the future, frustrated hater. It was this excruciating experience which forced me to demand the rule of work instead of the rule of friendship. I tried to turn the ideological and mystical belief in me into independent, practical accomplishment. I usually did not succeed. And this was a constant worry.

Most of the workers felt that either the technique of questioning or the peculiarities of the specific case were responsible for the problem. Only one educator hesitatingly mentioned that the audience had been "stiff" and "cold." Here are the notes I made after the meeting:

1. The mother was frank, wonderful; she broke down the barrier.

2. The group froze up more and more as the subject of genitality evolved, until the mother became confused and strained.

3. The discussion first tried to sidetrack the issue to such minor and superficial things as the method of questioning, the idea that the procedure had concentrated too much on the mother, the seats were too narrow, etc.

4. No contact could be made with the child. She refused to undress, and rightly so. The atmosphere was frigid.

5. The "people" had met the "specialists." The latter had failed.

6. The structural hatred came through with the force of machine-gun bullets.

7. It would be foolhardy to let these educators go out into the public to work with infant genitality.

8. No more children in the genital phase should be demonstrated for a while.

It had been clear to me for many years, and its general recognition stood out as our most essential task, that not one step toward basic preventive education could be taken unless the structural hatred, which exists generally in the human character, could be completely understood and mastered practically. Otherwise, every worker would again and again run into unrecognized danger and be unable to prevent disaster. It was also clear that, at the present time, it was far more important to overcome this terrible obstacle than to establish the natural laws of self-regulation, which are relatively simple to handle.

The audience had been frightened by the mother's frankness. Therefore, they "had heard too much about the mother." The seats had been too narrow because the students sitting on them had felt uncomfortably nervous. I had been unable to establish contact with the child and the child had refused to cooperate because one cannot easily function in the natural stream of life if there are people sitting around in a hostile manner, withdrawn, cold, "critical," haughty, inaccessible, inwardly fighting off anxiety and disgust with poorly disguised hostility. Then the living freezes up, draws back into the self, refuses to show its innermost core. Once again, it had become perfectly clear why the whole realm of genitality—infantile, pubertal, and adult—had been for so long shrouded in secrecy and surrounded by the taboo of "touch-it-not." The deep hatred against orgonomy, which persistently revealed these natural functions, was logical within this framework of armored man. The depth of the hatred seemed endless.

I now decided to bring all these issues into the open and risk destruction of the whole enterprise.

The following meeting, on February 19, 1950, began in a tense atmosphere. Everyone felt that the continued existence of the research group would be decided upon that day. I started by pointing out why I had waited more than ten years to call my coworkers together for the social task, despite numerous complaints that I had done nothing in the field of practical sociology since coming to the United States. My hesitancy was based on the conviction that no way had been found to cope with the structural fear and hatred of living functions, even within the most skilled and devoted workers in the field of orgonomy. Furthermore, whenever I pointed to some manifestation of this hatred, people thought it either peculiar or exaggerated or a personal whim or prejudice. For instance, when I had warned my students that the Brady attack in *Harper's** magazine was a red fascist smear, nobody believed me. They did not believe me again when this attack was pursued more openly in the then fellow traveler Wallace paper, *The New Republic*.† When I repeatedly pointed to all fascists' deep hatred against the living principle, people thought I felt resentment against the red fascists. Everyone refused to see the connection between general political pestilence

* Mildred Edie Brady, "The New Cult of Sex and Anarchy," *Harper's* (April 1947).

† "The Strange Case of Wilhelm Reich," *The New Republic* (May 26, 1947).

and individual structural hatred, which becomes accessible to medical scutiny.

When a biopsychiatrist of my experience has pointed out for decades that such a thing as the emotional plague exists within the structure of every educator, parent, physician, etc., it cannot be ignored with impunity. Over the years I had warned people not to run around making propaganda for sex-economy and the orgasm theory. The first task would have been to become aware, fully aware, of the depth and complexity of human misery. Motives for admiring my accomplishments were rarely rational. People became enthralled by what they saw as the promise of heaven on earth without any effort; of "orgastic potency" to be pinned on them without having to change the least bit in their basic ways of being and thinking; of the "great leader" who had finally given the answer to fascism of the black, red, and white varieties. But when fascism reared its ugly head right under the nose of the "Reichian" admirer, he stubbornly refused to see it. Under such conditions it was imperative to decline to lead anything or try to do anything at all in the ocean of human filth.

I told the workers of my desperate fight against the mystical expectations that swamped me and the dangers entailed in the inevitable disappointments that followed. I warned them that unless they learned to suffer from and for their educational tasks, they would not acquire the conviction and emotional strength to withstand the heavy blows which the emotional plague is capable of inflicting. When the truth about infant genitality has not penetrated anywhere; when it is killed every time it tries to make itself heard, there must be powerful factors at work against it. Therefore, naïveté was dangerous. True, I told them I could make them shout "Heil, Reich" at the top of their lungs. But this would not help a single child in a single difficulty. I wanted independent workers; workers who knew what they were doing; workers who would not cringe at the first sign of disapproval by some "authority"; workers who would be ready to abandon social or personal connections if these obligations contradicted their tasks as educators and physicians. I told them, too, that I did not care to be the leader of a group, or an association, or anything, if the group, the association, or what-not had no concrete purpose and task in the fight against the emotional plague. I had enough to do and had no ambition for formal leadership. Neither did I care for public recognition or honors of any kind; they were not worth much if they were not based on factual accomplishments. I had sacrificed my familial ties three times in order to be able to continue on my chosen path. I would certainly not abandon that path for some passer-by students or coworkers.

They were told to step out of the job if they could not adjust to the slow, toiling efforts required, with no awards to be expected. They would have to get rid of their adherence to erroneous public opinion. They would also have to become critical of the usual goings-on in the realm of child-rearing. This was no job for scared or suave little academicians. It was the toughest job ever taken on by physicians or educators. And last but not least, they would have to learn how to handle the armoring in children at its onset.

Armoring in a Newborn Infant

We assume that in a newborn infant an unwarped, highly plastic bioenergy system emerges from the womb and from then on it will be influenced by a multitude of environmental impacts, which will begin to form the infant's specific type of reaction to pleasure and to sorrow. Although prenatal damage will to a certain degree determine the manner in which postnatal stimuli are absorbed and structuralized, let us, for the sake of convenience, separate prenatal and postnatal development.

What matters here is whether or not and in what manner we can apply our base of operation in the specific, individual case. What obstacles do we encounter if we decide to *let only the interest of the child, and nothing else, determine the course of events?* The "nothing else" is, of course, exaggerated and not fully applicable in daily social life. We are aware that for centuries to come thwarted life will infringe upon healthy, newborn life and will cause more or less harm. However, it is crucial for the general line of procedure, as well as for the attainment of some degree of success in the OIRC, to learn to judge the obstacles to this undertaking as they arise in daily life. It seems best to conduct our inquiry with a specific case.

The mother of the infant to be discussed in the following pages was chosen from among a small group of applicants as one of the "fairly healthy" mothers. Biologically she appeared outgoing, direct, with no major twists in her character structure. She had been happily married for several years. Special requirements of her husband's job in the army had prevented them from having a baby, which they greatly desired. The mother was a pretty, sexually attractive woman of thirty. The first biophysical examination revealed a strong body, a warm radiating skin, sparkling eyes, full, sensuous lips, well-formed limbs and torso, relaxed and calm behavior.

She could express emotions of any kind freely, which is a major indication of free-flowing bioenergy. She could make ugly faces, sneer, growl, scream, show anxiety in her eyes, open her eyelids fully, wrinkle her forehead, bite and hit strongly with her fists at an imaginary hated object. The gag reflex was fully developed. Her eyes had a deep, serious, penetrating look full of contact, like the look of a deer.

The essential region in the examination of a future mother is, of course, the pelvis. I do not refer only to the mechanical factors, such as width of the entrance and exit of the pelvic bone structure, normal position of the uterus, absence of retroversion and prolapse, absence of trichomonas vaginalis, absence of cervical lacerations and erosions, of fibromatous and myomatous growths in the uterus, and regular and painless menstruations. These things are routine to any good obstetrician. *What matters here is whether or not there is any armoring in the pelvic segment.*

The reason for this is obvious: Pelvic armor precludes adequate orgastic discharge, reduces the vitality of the genital organs, and thus impedes full bioenergetic functioning of the fetus. In addition, it renders the total emotional system more vulnerable to strains and stresses of family difficulties, pregnancy disorders, and the delivery itself. We did not absolutely refuse mothers with armored pelvises, but we registered them in Group B, that is, with the intention of studying the existence or nonexistence of damage to the fetus growing in a spastic uterus; little is known about the influence of uterine spasm upon the fetus. The results had to be kept clearly separated, according to our basic distinctions between armored and unarmored organisms. We know from ample clinical evidence that if the pelvis is unarmored, the rest of the organism is also free of major immobility; and that if the pelvis is armored, armoring always exists in other segments of the organism. It was planned that one group of mothers in the OIRC, Group A, was to consist solely of those with free, unarmored pelvic segments.

To return to our mother: She enjoyed the genital embrace without fear or restriction. She could "let herself go" completely and had regular orgastic discharges; her whole bearing and expression corroborated this conclusion. Only a slight oversensitiveness in her middle abdominal segment could be found; it was easily removed.

In the psychological realm, there was an inclination toward an exaggeratedly idealistic attitude regarding motherhood and children. She beamed with the expectation of bearing a "healthy child," of raising it to manhood or womanhood in only joy and delight. She did not seem fully aware that bearing and rearing children is a major and often painful task. When this was mentioned to her, she appeared confident, in fact a bit *too* confident, regarding the job ahead. She also seemed to idealize her husband. They had, so she said, no conflicts at all; they were most happy together, etc. The examining physicians knew from reports by their chief social worker that not all was or seemed as rosy as the mother preferred to present it. The husband, a kind and handsome fellow, was inclined to verbal pornographic expressions. He had some set ideas about social and cultural matters which were not quite in agreement with his wife's biological structure. He also seemed to enjoy her idealization too much.

It is essential not to evaluate the parents in "absolute" terms of an "absolute" health with regard to an "absolutely healthy" child. On the contrary, such an attitude of absolute perfectionism causes much harm not only to the conduct of the parents but, of primary importance, to the preventive educational undertaking itself. The ideal of an "absolute" health and an "absolutely healthy" child contradicts the reality in which the child has to grow up. It most probably also contradicts the natural process itself, which never is and never can be perfect according to the ideals of man. The setting of absolute ideals in medicine or education precludes proper evaluation of what is and what is not possible to achieve. It will most likely break down at the first impact of a major obstacle.

In this particular instance, as in others, the mother and the social worker in charge of the case were in danger of failure because of this idea of absolute health. It is a general human character trait which we will be pondering about for quite some time. We shall realize later in what manner these characteristics of the mother actually began to exert their influence upon the infant in the *wrong* direction.

The staff which was to take care of the mother consisted of:

One physician, a medical orgonomist, whose task was to supervise the emotional status of the mother during pregnancy and to remove any blocking which might appear in any part of the organism.

Another medical orgonomist, who had specialized in the observation of small children and had had rich experiences with his own son, at that time four years old.

One orgonomically trained social worker. She was to be

in touch with the mother frequently enough to detect any emotional or physical deviation from the physiological.

One obstetrician, who was to deliver the baby; he was willing to cooperate with the OIRC in whatever was felt necessary to secure unimpeded development of the child.

Another medical orgonomist, who had performed a brilliant rescue in one delivery, was to stand by and to take charge in case of delay or complication of delivery.

The mother; she was to learn how much can be taught in groups to mothers about delivery and nursing.

One may ask at this point: Why this complicated machinery for the delivery of one baby? The answer is this: Since nothing whatsoever is known about the effects of bioenergetic and emotional disturbances on pregnancy and delivery, it was necessary to have as many skilled workers as possible standing by to observe and step in if necessary. It is of little use to have a psychologist who knows nothing about orgonotic streamings and a mechanically oriented obstetrician who delivers a baby, if it is the emotional development of the baby that is to be studied. It was necessary to have several orgonomically well-trained specialists pool their knowledge in order to miss as little as possible during the crucial period. Even divergences in opinions of the several observers could be expected to reveal major problems during the prenatal and the postnatal periods.

Reports on the behavior of the mother were obtained from different sources. In this manner, observations held in common could be distinguished from those which might reflect an individual emphasis. Also, the reactions of the different workers could be studied while they were in contact with the mother. For instance, one of the two social workers became severely disturbed when, during the first examination, the mother told the examining board that she enjoyed full genital gratification in the embrace. This social worker was at that time in a state of acute frustration, and she broke out crying. Thus we learned how the personal emotional status of a social worker can be affected by certain disclosures in a particular case. Such things of course happen wherever human life is handled medically or educationally. The good physician or social worker knows what goes on subterraneously in such contacts. The rigid, well-armored physician or social worker, on the other hand, does not know, or he discards it as "not belonging"; he may even get angry if such "personal interferences with the job" occur. Accordingly, the literature is bare of any inquiry into the role played by the emotional structures of the specialists involved.

Here is the report of the social worker some six weeks before the actual delivery:

> If you are interested in my personal impression of Mrs. L. and how she is carrying the baby, I can say I think it is excellent. Her whole attitude about her baby is remarkable compared to any of my previous experience. Her whole being seems saturated with happiness and contentment. She sits and radiates, and one feels good and close to the living in her presence. I feel very aware of the *baby* as though it were a member of the group. She doesn't seem anxious about anything. When discomfort or pain connected with childbirth is mentioned, she doesn't seem the least disturbed. When she learned that G.'s baby had died, she reacted warmly and sympathetically, but with no sign of identification or fear. She looks wonderfully healthy and has had no edema or negative physical symptoms, to my knowledge. She appears to have a good understanding of what the Orgonomic Infant Research Center is about and seems wholeheartedly for it.

Here is the report by the chief social worker, fifteen days after delivery:

Baby had its first bath on the eleventh day—seems to love it; gurgles and moves in the water. *Is startled if taken out of water too quickly (pulls shoulders back).*

Very active with head movements, is able to hold head up by itself; when held upright, moves head from side to side. Turns head and moves eyes according to sound and movements of people in the room. Appears to focus and coordinate eyes and follows objects as they move.

Has frequent hiccups, practically after every feeding. Also spits up milk; mother said this happens only when having bottle, but baby was observed by us to do it also after breast feeding.

Mother relates that at first the baby would suck very frequently (every hour) from breast. It would go to sleep at breast and start crying as soon as mother tried to put it back in crib. The bottle formula (which is given irregularly) was strengthened, and the baby calmed down and seemed to have needed added nourishment. *Mother realized she is tense at times, which is influencing the milk flow.* Baby at times sleeps for longer stretches during the night only if mother holds it in her arms. This tires mother out. Mother says baby likes breast better than bottle but takes to the bottle easily also. Baby gained 11 ounces the first week, 10½ ounces the second week. *Oral orgasm observed only during the first three days.* Baby still eats at least every three hours, usually more often.

Baby was observed by us while it was lying awake in its crib. Its color and body warmth were good at first; later, extremities seemed pale and cool. It started having hiccups, which lasted for quite some time. *Its chest seemed hard* ("bird cage"); *it would hold it in inspiration: inhalation long, exhalation short, staccato and irregular.* The baby

seemed restless on the whole. When having a bowel movement, the stool was loose and projectile—came out with a
terrific force, messing up the crib. Face became contorted,
pulled up legs. The father was "playfully" pulling its legs
and arms, which made baby seem even more uncomfortable. ("You be good or I'll punch your nose.")

The second report four days later reads as follows:

Baby's age: 19 days:
Baby has been having a cold for the last two days. The
breathing seemed obstructed; it was noisy and quick. *The
breathing has so far seemed to be reaching only the upper
chest, not down to the belly. The noisy breathing ceased
when it was sleeping peacefully in my arm for one half
hour; the chest was moving very rapidly, however.*

Generally the baby seemed restless, fretful, and unhappy.
Would be at the breast only for a short time; perspired
when sucking. (Often does, according to mother.) Holding
it would satisfy it only for a short while, then it would take
breast for a short period, then sleep for brief time, etc.
Usually its *crying was whimperish, rather weak.* Only once
did it really yell out with any force.

*Baby does not like to lie on belly but does sometimes lie
on its side.* At times it seems soothed by lying on its belly
over the mother's knee while having its back stroked.

Mother uses bottle frequently during the night; however,
the baby wants to sleep in mother's arms all night.

Mother stated that *caring for the baby was far more difficult than she had anticipated.* Had some kind of *a doll idea.*
It gives her anxiety and she feels at times at a loss as to
what to do to satisfy the baby. Mother says baby often
seems more restless at night and will cry, pulling up its legs
as if it had cramps (colic?).

Overall impressions: One difficulty with Mrs. L. is that
she has a *tendency to want to relate everything as "wonderful."* This was noted throughout the pregnancy: *It is an un-*

realistic, *Pollyannish attitude which covers up honest facts.*
She will usually only admit difficulties in the past tense.
The same holds true in her relationship with and perception of her husband. A consequence of this attitude is the
fact that the *mother now feels surprised and overburdened
by the demands of the baby.* She admits *she resents the
amount of time and energy she has to give to the baby, although she says this was only so in the beginning.* Furthermore, because everything is not just wonderful right now,
we can probably anticipate resentment on her part toward
the OIRC because we want the real facts.

Mr. L. appears to be somewhat lacking in sensitivity toward the baby. He manipulates its body rather roughly to
show it off and is in danger of taxing the baby beyond its
limits so that he can prove its "health." He is also rather
aggressive and dominating with his wife, who, however,
talks praisingly about her husband and says she is more in
love with him now than ever.

Mrs. L.'s mother-in-law continues to be present practically every day and also sleeps there nights, although she
does not live with the L.'s. According to Mrs. L., she has
worked out a very satisfactory arrangement with her
mother-in-law, who helps her with the housework and shop-
ping. Mrs. L. has been urged to handle the baby herself,
but from some of the things she says, *it seems that the
mother-in-law takes care of the baby a great deal too.*
Mrs. L. states that she could never have managed everything had it not been for her mother-in-law. Mrs. L. seems
definitely dependent upon the bottle; will she give up the
breast feedings for the bottle?

Summary: Something had gone wrong. The baby was
uncomfortable, and nobody seemed to know why. It was
only hinted that the mother did not seem to function too
well. The job of motherhood appeared to be far more
difficult for her than she had anticipated.

Was the mother not as well adjusted to her biological function as we had assumed? Or was there any other, hidden reason for the difficulty?

We know that such problems usually do not turn up in pediatric work. The child is given its chemical "routine shots." If the mother feels uncomfortable, she is advised to do this or that, to take it easy, to relax, to stick to a schedule, etc. To search for the roots of the trouble in a disturbance of the contact between mother and child is rarely thought of. A week later the following report came in from the chief social worker:

> I talked today with Dr. M., who saw the L.'s yesterday. He was not satisfied with Mrs. L., felt that she was tense, had anxiety; her eyes seemed dull. Dr. M. confirmed the impressions given in earlier reports. When Dr. M. questioned her, Mrs. L. admitted her difficulties in the past, but said that everything was all right *now*.

It was then decided to have the parents and the infant travel to Orgonon for a thorough examination of the situation. Clearly, it is far more important to learn all the details in a case such as this than to do research superficially with hundreds of babies. For a long time to come, the task must remain on a pilot research level. Further development proved this approach to be correct.

The parents brought the baby to Orgonon when it was five weeks and four days old. These were the basic points of the interview:

Q: Do you (mother) have contact with the baby?

A: Yes, frequently, but sometimes I don't.

Q: How do you know when you have no contact?

A: I don't seem to be able to be at ease with the baby— I don't seem to hold it the right way, and then the baby does not seem comfortable, it becomes anxious and un-happy.

The mother had contact with the baby most of the time, but she also knew when she had lost contact. Here the first dangerous miscomprehension of "health" manifested itself:

The mother seemed *to feel guilty about not being a "healthy" mother, about not fulfilling her task in the OIRC* when her contact with the baby was poor. And the baby apparently responded to the lack of contact with discom-fort. What then was wrong here? The temporary lack of contact, or the guilt feeling about not having contact? Obviously the latter. *It is natural that a mother at times loses contact with her child for a brief period.* It is a sign of an alert and alive structure to *know when* contact is lack-ing. To have guilt feelings about it does not seem to belong here. Why should a mother feel guilty if she tem-porarily has no contact? And what do such guilt feelings do to her organism, and through her organism, to the baby?

Such questions bother mothers all over the world. The orgonotic sense of contact, a function of the orgone energy field of both the mother and the child, is unknown to most specialists; however, the old country doctor knew it well.

Orgonotic contact is the most essential experiential and emotional element in the interrelationship between mother and child, particularly prenatally and during the first days and weeks of life. The future fate of the child depends on it. It seems to be the core of the newborn infant's emotional development. We know very little about it yet. Let us, therefore, explore it further.

The next problem in the interview was to find out *what the disturbed contact did to the child.*

INTERVIEWER: It is to be expected that the child will feel uncomfortable if your contact is absent. The important point is that you clearly know *when* you do *not* have contact. An armored mother most likely would not know it, and thus could not change the situation. Let me ask you a few questions to find out:

1. Why you lose contact
2. How you yourself react to the loss of contact
3. What happens to the baby when you lose contact.

How do you know what the baby wants when it cries?

MOTHER: It cries differently according to what it wants. I have learned how to distinguish it. At times I am not sure; I then try different things until I have found out what it wants.

INTERVIEWER: You are right there. With full contact established, the mother knows what the baby wants. But we must get away from the idea that everything should be *perfect*, that you should have contact *all* the time, that the baby must *always* be happy and healthy. The main thing is not whether or not the child at times feels uncomfortable but whether or not you know why it suffers and can pull yourself and the baby out of it. Health in other respects also does not consist in never being unhappy or always being healthy, but, basically, in whether or not the organism is capable of pulling out of unhappiness and illness. These ideals about an "absolute happiness" and "health" should be given up outright. They are mystical, no good, and cause much harm. It is to your credit as a well-functioning mother that you are aware of your own occasional depressions. Do you know why you get depressed?

MOTHER: At times I feel strongly that I am tied down, overburdened by caring for the baby. I did not know when I expected the baby that it would mean so much hard work.

INTERVIEWER: It is quite natural for a young, lively mother to feel the burden and to resent it at times. You cannot go dancing whenever you'd like to, and your time is not quite your own. It is also natural that in your joyful expectation of having a baby you overrated the pleasure and underestimated the burden you would have to carry. It would be very strange if you did *not* feel resentment against the baby at times. However, to block off those feelings and be unaware of these human attitudes would constitute a serious danger to yourself and to the baby, emotionally. Therefore, do not worry about losing contact or disliking the baby from time to time. However, I feel that there is more to it. Don't you feel that you do not quite live up to the demand of being a "healthy mother"? Don't you feel that a *"healthy"* mother should have a *"perfect"* baby and should *never* be depressed or distressed?

MOTHER *(her eyes suddenly brightening and her face flushing):* Oh, yes, I feel burdened by the obligation to be always healthy and perfect. I feel that I do not comply with the expectations people have in this case with regard to the baby.

INTERVIEWER: Now this is critical. In addition to the natural reaction against being tied down by the baby, you feel obliged to comply with certain expectations as to health and perfect behavior. This is an unnecessary depression. It is bad for you and bad for the baby. Who expects so much of you?

MOTHER: Being one of the "healthy mothers" under the care of the OIRC, I feel I must not fail as a mother. This depresses me. My husband always boasts of what a healthy baby we have, but this is not quite true. My baby is not quite healthy. I know it and I do not know why. I do my best and it does not quite work. My baby had a cold when it was two weeks old, and since then it has not been well, although the cold is long gone.

INTERVIEWER: We shall go into that very soon. First your husband. *(To the father)* Do you have contact with the baby? Do you like it?

FATHER: I love it . . . The baby always smiles at me; I have good contact . . . *(There was a peculiar ring in the father's statement about the smile.)*

INTERVIEWER: What do you mean by "it always smiles at me"? Why should it?

FATHER: I pull the baby's legs, make it stretch, make certain sounds it likes . . .

(Why should the father stretch the baby's legs?)

INTERVIEWER: You should not experiment with the baby. Do what the baby wants, but do not do things with the baby only because *you* like it. Just be with the baby. Enjoy it, don't "watch" it for watching's sake. Stay in the background . . .

(The mother confirmed that she had to stop the father at times.)

INTERVIEWER: Do many people come to visit your home? Do they interfere with your procedures? What about your mother?

MOTHER: People come at times to see the baby, but I do not let them handle the baby. My mother-in-law helps out . . .

(The eyes of the mother went blank at this moment.) She was asked what her relationship to her mother-in-law was like. The experienced orgonomist could not have failed to notice the change in the mother's behavior. She seemed blocked in her expression; she paled. Then, very hesitantly, she said that very often she had to assert herself against her mother-in-law, to tell her to stop commanding and to let her decide herself. She complained that the grandmother's expression and "touch" with the baby were not always right.

She was advised to keep the grandmother away from the child more and, if she felt that the infant suffered, to handle it herself without the grandmother's assistance. She should let herself be guided in this matter by whether or not the child felt comfortable and by nothing else. As long as the child enjoyed contact with the grandmother, it was all right.

The mother then said that circumcision of newborn male infants meant a great deal to the people in the neighborhood and to her relatives in the small town where the L.'s lived. Family and neighbors could not understand why the child was *not* circumcised. Circumcision seemed to have a peculiar meaning to all those people who had insisted that the baby should be circumcised. It was as if the child's circumcision would serve a strong emotional need in the grownups, rather than any other consideration.

The situation had been especially complicated with the mother's parents. She had not had the courage to tell them that the child had not been circumcised; she had told them that the child *had* been circumcised "in order to have peace." The mother sees her parents only very rarely and she assured us that they would have no influence on the child. Still, it remained a puzzle why she had not told the truth. We can see clearly that without the connection with the OIRC the mother would have yielded to her parents' expectations and a severe injury would have been inflicted upon the child.

The question now arose as to whether the parents wanted the child to grow up as a Jew. The mother declared that she did *not;* she thought it immaterial since those national boundaries were artificial. The father insisted that he was conscious of being a Jew and he could not see any reason why the child should reject the fact that he too was a Jew as he was growing up. He planned to teach the child about his Jewish ancestors and traditions so that he would become a "good Jew," conscious of his heritage from Judaism.

Here a conflict appeared to be developing between the

father and the mother with regard to a major question concerning the child's future. It was well known to the interviewers that such conflicts are apt to confuse the child, to cause conflict in its double dependence on father and mother; that the party which lost this fight would resent it and feel subdued by the other. Here, the rationale and efficiency of the OIRC's base of operations was to be tested. The conflict between the parents, the mother being more world-minded and the father more nationalistically inclined, could only be solved by the "third factor," the common functioning principle, i.e., the *interest of the child and nothing but the child*. Accordingly, the physician tried to explain the standpoint of the OIRC.

The mother as well as the father had of course a full right to their own feelings and opinions. However, the counseling physician felt that the mother represented the interest of the child more completely than the father. The mother's standpoint still left the opportunity open for the child to decide later whether or not it wanted to be a Jew. The father's view, on the other hand, left the child no choice but would force it right from the beginning, when it could not defend itself, into a certain cultural and religious pattern which the child, deep down, might resent and want to reject.

Would the father, as fathers were accustomed to do some decades ago and still are wont to do, determine *in advance* whether the child should become a carpenter or a lawyer? The father said that he would of course never try to do such a thing. Then why determine right now whether the child should grow up as a Jew? At first the father could not see the point. It seemed to him that being a Jew was different from being a carpenter. He believed that Judaism is somehow inherited, given by birth. The physician denied this. He said that children were born neither Jews nor car-

penters nor anything else; that it was the environment with
its preconceived ideas which thought that way. The child
was born as nothing more than a plastic bioenergetic system, ready to pick up anything from the environment that
was imprinted on its organism with some degree of persistence. To force it to be a Jew would not serve the child's
development to independence and self-regulation, which
both parents were willing to secure. Just as forced circumcision represents a most violent interference with the inborn freedom of a person, the early determination of what
a child should or should not be or become violates the
child's rights by forcing it at its most plastic age into a
certain preconceived direction. Judaism is all right for whoever wants it. Judaism must be respected as any other belief
held by people must be respected. There is nothing wrong
with Judaism so long as it does not interfere with the rights
of infants and their natural development. If the child, during its later development, tended toward Judaism, this
would be perfectly all right; it would then be the child's
own choice. But not now or during the first five to ten years
of its life. It may later want to join the Catholic Church or
the Mohammedan faith or worship nature or feel free to
just enjoy the world. The father's standpoint had nothing
to do with the child's interest, which alone should determine its growth. This was the basic policy of the OIRC. No
interest in state, culture, religion, nationality, etc., should
be permitted to influence the child's development. Even
the state gives its citizens the full right to determine where
they want their children born, and even whether or not
they want to be citizens, except, of course, in the lands of
the "liberators." Otherwise, the concept and meaning of
freedom and self-regulation would be lost and it would
have been worthless from the start.

The father seemed now to realize the standpoint of the

OIRC, but emotionally he still adhered to his personal view. He promised to think matters over and to report later on what conclusion he reached.

BEGINNING OF ARMORING AT
THE AGE OF FIVE WEEKS

We have learned in orgonomic medicine that most basic functions of biopathies begin to develop prenatally and immediately after birth. The psychological approach, including the psychoanalytic, can reach only to the age where language forms, i.e., to about the third year of life. Before this age one must rely on the *expressive, emotional language* and on the *orgonotic contact* one can establish with the infant's living system.

The infant we were studying confirmed the fact that it is necessary to penetrate to this deeper wordless level to get at the source of armoring. He had developed bronchitis in his second week. Such happenings are usually registered under a heading like "cold" or "sniffles," which "will pass by in due time with no further consequences." In orgonomy we proceed differently. We ask:

1. Why a cold should develop at all
2. Whether any bioenergetic functions are involved in the cold
3. What the possible consequences of such an early cold are for the biophysical functioning of the infant.

Our infant was pale; its upper chest was "quiet." The breathing was noisy, and the chest did not seem to move properly with respiration. The expiration was shallow. Bronchial noises could be heard on auscultation. Generally the infant appeared uncomfortable. Instead of crying loudly, it whimpered. It moved little and looked ill.

First, we had to establish whether this restriction of respiration had immediately followed the cold. The mother confirmed that the child had had these "noises in the chest" ever since the onset of the "cold." It was clear that the chest had never quite relaxed since.

On examination of the chest, the intercostal muscles felt hard. The child seemed oversensitive to touch in this region. The chest as a whole had not yet hardened, but it was held in inspiration with the upper part bulging forward. No physician trained only in classical ways would have thought that anything was wrong.

Upon slight stimulation of the intercostal muscles the chest softened but did not yield fully when pressed down. The infant immediately started to move vigorously. The breathing cleared up appreciably, and the child began to sneeze (bursts of sudden *expiration*), smiled, then coughed several times vigorously, and finally urinated. The relaxation increased visibly; the back, formerly arched, curved forward and the cheeks reddened. The noisy breathing stopped. The mother was instructed that this first blocking of respiration was not too serious, but that it would recur. She should learn to bring the chest down *herself* whenever the blocking of respiration occurred, by gentle tickling stimulation of the intercostal chest muscles. The infant was able to relinquish the blocking itself after the "first aid" had been rendered; therefore, the blocking could not be considered chronic at that point. But the parents were told to watch out that the chest rigidity did not become chronic; it should be removed whenever it appeared.

Theoretically, this was a major new insight into early armoring in infants. The "cold" itself could be understood as the result of a contraction (sympathetic reaction) of the organism due to lack of contact with the mother. Such a contraction necessarily causes paleness, lowering of the peripheral bioenergetic charge and the body temperature, and centers in the chest as bronchitis, i.e., sympathetic irritation of the bronchi with increased mucus secretion. Thus *a general bioenergetic disturbance is at the source of the local somatic symptom.* The latter in turn will increase the bioenergetic contraction and impede full expiration. This will cause anxiety and nervousness, which in turn will make it more difficult for the baby to establish full contact with the mother. The mother, burdened with conflict and bad conscience, as well as rebellion, will not quite succeed in establishing full contact with the infant. Thus, the vicious circle is established closing the cycle from first contraction, to a "cold," to inability to establish contact, to new colds, to restriction of expiration, to lack of sleep, to annoyance on the part of the mother, to irrational behavior, and so forth. This kind of vicious circle most likely constitutes the core around which biopathic noxae later gather like layers around a shell. It is these layers that we have to peel off in adult biopathies.

The individual somatic disease symptom now appears merely as a small cog in the big machine called "biopathy." The "cold" has its origin in a bioenergetic, i.e., emotional disturbance of energy equilibrium, and not in innocent "air germs" or unseen viruses. The "cold" in infants is an immediate expression of an irritation of the mucous membranes of the respiratory tract due to disequilibrium of energy metabolism because of lack of orgonotic contact. Later on, chronically irritated mucous membranes may well function independently of any emotional irritation. The bioenergetic disturbance becomes structuralized somatically in a "disposition to colds."

These new insights are of the utmost importance in many ways:

First, we obtain a valuable weapon with which we can get at the background of chronic diseases. What is generally called "disposition to disease" appears now as tangible restrictions of bioenergetic functioning in early infancy.

Second, we have learned that the orgonotic contact between mother and infant is of primary importance for an understanding of as well as for coping medically with early mishaps, which have previously been unrecognized.

Third, we are beginning to learn to read the language of the infant's emotional expression, a most hopeful prospect. Thus we can hope with some degree of certainty that the fog now surrounding early infant diseases will slowly disappear.

It should be stated plainly that this is only a very crude beginning. It will take many decades and many workers in the field to master the onset of disease in early infancy.

The infant was brought back the next day for a demonstration before some thirty physicians, educators, social workers, and laboratory workers. The rough respiration had returned to some extent. It was quite easy to remove the blocking this time, and the child was able to scream loudly, whereas before it had only whimpered feebly.

Ten days later the following report was received from our chief social worker:

The mother related that the baby was "blossoming" since it had been brought to Orgonon. It had slept peacefully all the way home; formerly it could sleep only for very brief periods of time. It now sometimes sleeps all through the night or at least six to eight hours at a time. It eats with great vigor and cries heartily. When awake it smiles and "talks" frequently. The mother now is fully aware of the orgonotic interaction between herself and the baby. She feels well and confident. She does not suffer from loss of contact, and the baby reacts with great pleasure to the bodily contact. The crying of the baby is much more forceful than before. It is also much more "demanding." If its needs are not attended to immediately when it cries, however, its body tenses up and turns red, and it arches its back and holds its breath.

The breathing continues to be noisy, usually when it is actively moving and kicking, not at all when it is sleeping. The mother tries successfully to stroke the chest gently downward when the chest gets fixed in an inspiratory position, or to tickle gently the intercostal spaces in the sides of the chest. The baby likes it. The body gives way; it "caves in." But this has no immediate effect on the noisy breathing. In general, the mother believes the chest still is somewhat high and held in inspiration. At times the breathing still impressed me as "desperate."

The early blocking of respiration seemed to gain importance rapidly as more children were observed. Somehow the diaphragmatic region appeared to respond first and most severely to emotional, bioenergetic discomfort. In the case of this particular infant, the early bronchitis had complicated and helped to maintain the respiratory block for an unusually long period of time. The infant was apparently on its way toward chronic armoring in the diaphragmatic region. However, it was hoped that continuous vigilance with regard to the noisy breathing which resulted from the respiratory blocking, and first aid applied as soon as possible *by the mother,* would finally remove the threat of chronic armoring in the chest completely. With it, a certain form of "disposition" would be eliminated.

After this case, close attention was paid to the early history of armored small children in order to determine

whether or not respiratory blocking is a preferred mechanism of emotional disturbances in infancy. It seemed entirely possible that a preference for diaphragmatic blocking
in early infancy has some relation to the intense emotional
excitability of the central *plexus coeliacus,* which is located
in the diaphragmatic segment. Other blockings would then
be expected to spread upward and downward over the
organism. This outlook, now to be carefully studied, held
great promise for early prevention of biopathic conditions.

Three weeks later the attending medical orgonomist
reported that the baby was doing very well. It had doubled
its weight and looked large for its age (the parents were of
rather small stature). The baby was now plump with a
healthy pink color. It moved constantly and vigorously;
this appeared to be the outstanding impression. According
to the physician's report, the baby's face seemed to reflect
its actions. Its expression changed continuously from
strength, to intensity, to softness, to smiles, etc. It often
made pleasurable sounds and seemed fully aware of what
was going on around it. Generally, the baby now appeared
vigorous, active, and happy.

But the noisy breathing was still noticeable most of the
time. It stopped only when the baby became less active.
The mother had learned to get the chest down in a playful
way when it became fixed high in inspiration. The baby
seemed to enjoy the mother's help; it "caved in" and showed
happiness, but this had no apparent effect on the noisy
breathing. Neither did it seem to have a lasting effect on
the chest as such, which after a while returned to its high
position. The abdomen felt slightly hard; it softened only
when the baby was feeding.

However, the baby's sounds and crying were much freer
and fuller than they had been three weeks ago, before first

aid was rendered. Then, as we recall, it was whimperish and staccato. He also sleeps for long stretches and eats regularly about every four hours. He eats all kinds of strained fruit, drinks juices, and takes vitamins. Bowel movement is regular once a day. Sometimes the lips quiver in oral orgasm after feeding. The mother takes the baby into the orgone energy accumulator once or twice daily for three to five minutes. He seems to have had enough by then; he becomes restless. His body flushes strongly in the accumulator, without perspiration. The mother uses the accumulator regularly herself; she has a "sinking, open" feeling while in it and feels that respiration becomes fuller.

Thus the report of the assistant physician. A first substantial result seems to have been obtained. The baby has greatly improved. It remains to be seen how and when the first injury it has suffered will turn up again or become worse. From now on, however, it can be met with a bit of firm knowledge, which further experience will extend. One thing appears certain: *No absolutes in terms of "health" can be applied.* Rational infant-rearing deals with many big and small problems which turn up and must be handled skillfully. The armored parent will not sense the trouble, or, sensing it, will be helpless, lacking immediate orgonotic contact. The fairly mobile parent will sense the trouble and, in some cases, be able to render first aid. In most cases the trouble will remain untouchable due to lack of knowledge. The necessary knowledge in early infant care must be acquired bit by bit from many experiences and observations. A long and arduous task, indeed. But the only one that carries some promise.

The problem of how much of these fine and most spontaneous activities in a wordless human interrelationship which resists verbal expression can be taught to mothers, fathers, nurses, and doctors at large remains unsolved. It is hoped that this question, too, will eventually find its proper answer, provided patience and careful unprejudiced study are maintained. But the admonition not to create from all this a new ideal of "perfect" orgonotic contact between mother and child appears essential. Let mothers just enjoy their babies and the contact will develop spontaneously.

Falling Anxiety in a
Three-Week-Old Infant

I recently had the opportunity to observe the development of falling anxiety in a three-week-old infant. This observation filled a gap in my investigation of the cancer biopathy.

The infant in question was born into an environment in which the expressive language of the organism is professionally understood and used. It was, therefore, all the more disconcerting that the parents felt helpless when confronted with the gesture language of an infant. They had the impression that *nothing at all is known about the emotional life of the newborn child.* The *emotional* needs of the infant are, of course, in no way satisfied by purely mechanical care, which is given in response to only *one* form of communication, namely, *crying.* This one form covers countless large and small needs, from the irritation of a diaper crease to colic. The infant's other modes of expression meet with no response from the environment.

I shall refrain from discussing here those damaging kinds of infant care that modern education has already eliminated from the world or is still combating: the rigid apportioning of food and inflexible adherence to feeding times à la Pirquet; forcible extension of the legs by tight swaddling; denial of the breast during the first twenty-four hours, as still practiced in many hospitals; overheating of nurseries; the routine treatment of infants in large institu-

114

tions; the practice of letting infants "cry themselves out," etc. Such compulsive measures express the parents' and physicians' inimical attitudes toward life. Their effect is immediate postnatal damage to the biological self-regulation of the organism, creating the basis for a later biopathy, which is then misinterpreted as hereditary taint. All this is known today, even though it may not yet have had an impact on common practices in child care.

I would like to limit myself here to one specific damaging influence in the first weeks of life that has been neglected until now: *the lack of orgonotic contact, of a direct physical or psychological nature, between the infant and the person who takes care of it.* The capacity to understand the infant's language of emotional expression depends directly upon the closeness of this contact; the more complete the orgonotic contact, the better the understanding.

The most salient place of contact in the infant's body is the bioenergetically highly charged mouth and throat. This body organ reaches out immediately for gratification. *If the nipple of the mother reacts to the infant's sucking movements in a biophysically normal manner with sensations of pleasure, it will become strongly erect and the orgonotic excitation of the nipple will become one with that of the infant's mouth, just as in the orgastically gratifying sexual act, in which the male and female genitals luminate and fuse orgonotically.* There is nothing "abnormal" or "disgusting" in this. Every healthy mother experiences the sucking as pleasure and yields to it.

However, about 80 percent of all women suffer from vaginal anesthesia and frigidity. Their nipples are correspondingly anorgonotic, i.e., "dead." The mother may develop anxiety or loathing in response to what would naturally be a sensation of pleasure aroused in the breast by the infant's sucking. This is why so many mothers do not want to nurse their babies. Furthermore, an anorgonotic breast functions poorly physiologically; i.e., milk production is disturbed. The excited mouth of the infant thus encounters either a "dead" nipple, so that it experiences no satisfaction, or the nonexcitable rubber nipple of a bottle, to which the mother, because of her phobia, has restricted the infant.

The impairment of plasmatic functioning in the mouth and the neck and shoulder regions that we find in biopathies leaves no doubt that severe damage to the infant's orgonity in the region of the head and neck is caused by these disturbances in the mother. Speech disorders, lack of emotional expression, spasms of the neck muscles, eating disturbances, spastic hysterical vomiting, fear of kissing, depression, stuttering, mutism, etc., are consequences of poor orgonotic functioning of the mouth and neck organs. So much for the infant's first physiological contact with the world.

Let us now proceed to emotional contact, which is determined directly by orgonotic contact. The infant has no means of expression at his disposal other than various forms of movement (grimaces, movements of the arms, legs, and torso, expressions of the eyes) and crying. The mother grasps the expression of the infant's gestures at first through orgonotic contact (in psychological terms, through identification). If her own organism is free and emotionally expressive, she will understand the infant. But if she is armored, characterologically hard, timid, or otherwise inhibited, she will fail to understand the infant's language and therefore the emotional development of the child will be exposed to a variety of damaging influences. The infant's needs can be satisfied only if its expressions are understood. But exactly what the infant wants is not always easy to know.

Every newborn child has its individuality, its own *emotional keynote*, which must be recognized if its individual emotional reactions are to be comprehended. The infant in this particular case of falling anxiety was characterized by an "earnest-looking" expression. This "looking" expression was fully developed just a few minutes after birth; i.e., the newborn baby's eyes were wide open and gave the impression of "seeing." He took the breast immediately and vigorously. During the first week he did not cry very much. In the second week, however, he cried frequently, and none of the people looking after him was able to figure out what was causing him to cry. The pacifier did not always quiet him, and I often had the sense that the child wanted something *quite definite*. But what? It was two weeks before I understood that what he wanted was *body contact*. I will have to explain this point.

During the few hours the baby was awake, his eyes followed the winding red lines painted on the wall of his room. Red was clearly preferred over blue and green. The infant's gaze would stay much longer on the red, with a much more intense expression in his look.

At the age of two weeks, the infant experienced his first orgastic excitation of the mouth. It happened while he was sucking: the eyeballs turned upward and sideways, the mouth began to tremble, the tongue quivered. Then the contractions spread over the whole face. After about ten seconds they subsided and the musculature of the face relaxed. This excitation seemed perfectly natural to the parents, but we know from experience that many parents become alarmed when their child experiences oral orgasm. In the following four weeks, these convulsive movements occurred several times.

At the end of his third week of life, the infant experienced an attack of acute falling anxiety as he was being taken from his bath and placed on his back upon a table. It was not immediately apparent whether the movement of laying him down had been too fast or whether the cooling of the skin had brought about the falling anxiety. Whatever the cause, *the child began to cry violently, stretched his arms backward as though to gain support, tried to bring his head forward, showed sheer panic in his eyes, and could not be quieted.* He had to be picked up. As soon as the attempt was again made to lay him down, the falling anxiety reappeared just as violently. He could be calmed only by being held.

For the following few days his right shoulder blade and right arm were pulled back and less mobile than his left arm. The contraction of the right shoulder musculature was quite distinct, and its connection with the falling anxiety was clear. *During the anxiety attack the child had drawn back both shoulders as if to keep himself from falling. This muscular attitude persisted; it failed to relax even during periods free of anxiety.*

I now attach great significance to this incident. However, the following explanations for it can be excluded:

It could not be a question of genital orgasm anxiety of the type that occurs after puberty. Nor could it be a rational fear, since a three-week-old infant has no concept of "falling" or of "height" or "depth." It also could not be a case of psychoneurotic falling anxiety, since there are no concepts before the development of word language and there can be no phobia without concepts.

The psychoanalytic explanation of "instinct anxiety" usually offered in such cases is not satisfactory. For the question would then be: What kind of ego instinct was being warded off? There is no such thing as a moral ego at this age and, according to psychoanalytic theory, where there is no moral defense there can be no instinct anxiety.

There is no "ego" to "signal" an instinctual breakthrough with the anxiety attack.

Rationalistic as well as psychological explanations, therefore, provide no answer. *How is it possible for an acute anxiety attack to occur in a three-week-old infant who possesses neither consciousness of the danger of falling nor an instinctive defense signal of the ego against anxiety?* Recourse to the notion of an "archaic, inborn, instinct anxiety" would be plain laziness and prove nothing at all. *An anxiety attack is a functional disturbance and can be understood only in terms of the orgonotic body functions.*

Let us attempt a biophysical interpretation: If the fear of danger and the defense against an instinct are to be excluded, *what remains is the pleasure-anxiety mechanism of the orgonotic body system,* which functions with the very first stirring of the plasma. In *Psychischer Kontakt und vegetative Strömung* (1934)* I had to make the assumption that *the sensation of falling is a purely biophysical occurrence brought about by a rapid withdrawal of the biological energy from the periphery to the vegetative center of the organism.* It is the same type of kinesthetic organ sensation that occurs in actual falling, in fright, and when orgastic expansion is suddenly inhibited. As I have shown clinically, falling anxiety is always at the root of orgasm anxiety. *The rapid and extreme pulsation of orgasm is experienced as falling if it cannot run its course unimpeded.* By contrast, the uninhibited orgastic contraction conveys the sensation of floating or flying.

The withdrawal of bioenergy from the body periphery represents an anorgonia† of the extremities. Loss of the

---

* Chapter XIII in *Character Analysis.*

† The concept of anorgonia encompasses those biopathic conditions that share one common source, namely, *a block in plasma motility.* See *The Cancer Biopathy,* Chapter IX.

sense of equilibrium accompanies the anorgonia of the supporting organs.

Falling anxiety is therefore not a "psychic formation" but the simple expression of sudden anorgonia in those organs that maintain the equilibrium of the body by *opposing* the pull of gravity. Whether falling anxiety and anorgonia are induced by the sudden onset of orgasm anxiety, by real falling, or by a fright contraction, the mechanism remains the same: *loss of peripheral plasma motility, accompanied by loss of the sense of equilibrium and of equilibrium itself.* The experience of anxiety is an immediate biophysical reaction to sudden contraction of the plasma system. The orgonotic contraction, however, is connected with *the loss of plasma motility at the periphery and, for this reason, manifests itself as the fear of falling.*

Whether the immobilization occurs as a result of a secondary blocking of pleasure or because of a primary anxiety contraction is a matter of indifference. The effect is the same: *the falling sensation is the immediate inner perception of the immobilization of the body periphery and the loss of equilibrium.* The body's balance in the gravitational field is therefore a function of the full orgonotic pulsation at the periphery of the orgonotic system.

I must relate an incident that supports this interpretation. A boy I knew had caught a squirrel and was holding it in his hand. I was struck by the fact that the squirrel lay completely limp in his hand, without struggling, without biting, and without wriggling, indeed, without moving at all. It was completely paralyzed with fright, and was suffering an acute anorgonotic attack. After a few minutes the boy put the squirrel on the ground. At first it lay there as though dead, i.e., completely motionless. Then it tried to get up but fell down. In terms of physics, it could not overcome the pull of gravity. Its attempts to get back on its legs remained unsuccessful for about fifteen minutes. Yet it was not hurt, for later it ran and climbed very well. The disturbance of the sense of equilibrium and the continuous falling down produced increasing anxiety and caused more falling. For several minutes the squirrel convulsed in sudden contractions that were so strong it was thrown 10 to 20 cm. into the air. Finally, the animal recovered from the attack and crawled into a bush, where it rested for a long time before scampering away.

Let us now return to our infant. Is it possible to infer a cause of the anorgonotic attack? I think so. *For about the first two weeks the mother's orgonotic contact with the baby had been poor.* The child had obviously had strong impulses for body contact that had not been satisfied. Then the oral orgasm occurred, a completely natural discharge of the high-pitched excitation in the head and throat region. This increased the need for contact still further. The lack of contact led to a contraction, a withdrawal of biological energy as a consequence of vain efforts to establish the contact. If it were appropriate to use the terminology of psychology here, we would say that the child "resigned" (that it was "frustrated"). However, the "biological resignation" brought on the anorgonia, and the falling anxiety appeared.

I succeeded in my attempts to overcome the falling anxiety in the infant. Assuming that my conclusions were correct, I found the following three procedures necessary:

1. *The infant had to be picked up and held when he cried.* That helped, and the falling anxiety ceased to occur after about three weeks. Fear of strangers had appeared with the falling anxiety. Before the first attack, the child would happily go into the arms of every stranger; after the attack, he would begin to cry in fear. He had also reacted once with anxiety to the sudden appearance of a dog.

2. *His shoulders, fixed in a "backward" position, had to be gently moved forward, in order to eliminate this first onset of a characterological armoring in them.* I accomplished this playfully, laughing and making sounds the child loved. This was continued on a daily basis for about two months, always as if in play.

3. *The child actually had to be "allowed to fall" in order to let him get used to the sensation of falling.* He would be held under the armpits and gently raised and then lowered, at first slowly, then increasingly quickly. At first he reacted by crying, but in time began to enjoy the movements. Soon he developed a game out of this routine of being lifted up and then lowered. When he was able to hold himself upright, he began to make "walking movements" with his legs. He leaned against my chest and looked up at my head. I understood. *He wanted to climb up on me.* Once he arrived at the top of my head, he squealed for joy. In the weeks that followed, the climbing and "falling" became a favorite game.

Fortunately, the first biopathic reaction was overcome. During the next six months we did not see any trace of the falling anxiety.

It is important to follow the development of this infant in an area that is directly connected with biopathic shrinking: *If the carcinomatous shrinking of the adult organism is rooted in chronic contraction and resignation acquired at an early age, it can be concluded that the prevention of the shrinking biopathy is dependent on the undisturbed development of the vital impulses in the first months of life.*

It would no doubt be simpler and more popular if a drug against the shrinking process in cancer could be developed, but since this is not possible, we have no alternative but to concentrate on *the sex-economic upbringing of the newborn infant.* So far as I can see, there is no other way, despite the serious social implications that this course of action involves.

We started with the adult's lack of understanding of the expressive language of newborn infants. This lack is far-reaching and quite general. The parents of the infant in this case believed themselves to be especially understanding when they allowed the newborn infant to decide for himself when his feeding times should be and how much nourishment he should take. But as early as the fourth week of the child's life, they noticed a distress that manifested itself in repeated crying. At first, they did not understand. Slowly the simple realization dawned on them that it is extremely dreary to lie all alone in a crib for hours at a time, day after day, with high walls on both sides and a cover over the top.

The aliveness of the newborn infant requires aliveness of its surroundings. Infants prefer vibrant colors to gray or dull tones, and moving objects to stationary ones. If the infant is set in his carriage so that its sides no longer obstruct his view, and if the top is removed, he can see everything around him without difficulty and will show a lively interest in the people passing by, in the trees, shrubs, posts, walls, and so on.

The concept of the "autism of the child," of his "being withdrawn into himself," is as erroneous as it is widespread. The autism of the infant is an artifact caused by the behavior of the adults. It is generated by the strict isolation of the infant and by the characterological armoring of the adults responsible for his care and also of the theoreticians of child care. The infant will quite understandably not emerge from himself—or will do so only with the greatest difficulty—if only inflexible rules and ungenuine behavior are extended to him rather than living warmth.

It is perfectly true that today most newborn infants are

quiet and withdrawn into themselves. But is lordosis or anxiety neurosis natural just because it is common? As long as parents, doctors, and educators approach infants with false, unbending behavior, inflexible opinions, condescension, and officiousness, instead of with orgonotic contact, infants will continue to be quiet, withdrawn, apathetic, "autistic," "peculiar," and, later, "little wild animals," whom the cultivated feel they have to "tame."

This world will not change, despite all the political talk, as long as grownups fail to take the trouble to prevent their own deadness from exercising an influence on the still unspoiled plasma system of the infant.

An infant does not respond with any expressive movement to honey-sweet "baby talk" or to words of strictness by adults. *He responds only to the intonation and pitch of a voice, to a language that is related to his own.* In an infant just a few weeks old, it is possible to educe glowing pleasure and lively responses by talking to him in *his* guttural sounds, and making *his* movements, and, above all, by maintaining a lively contact with him. False behavior on the part of the grownup inevitably forces the child back into himself. It cannot be emphasized enough that in this particular matter ninety percent of all adults are still completely unaware, and because of this, biopathic constitutions are being produced every day.

Deficiencies of inner secretion and of the highly interesting enzyme functions are the *results* and *symptoms, not* the causes, of later diseases of the biosystem. This must be correct if the mechanical-chemical viewpoint of biology is incorrect—*and it is incorrect.* The miserable state of health of the population of this planet is sufficient proof of this point.

The horrendous way Indians, Japanese, or many other authoritarian Asiatics bring up small children should not be too great a surprise to us. We are not much better here in the "cultured" West. Only the methods of "taming the wild little animals" are different. The old-spinster spirit, intolerant of anything alive in its vicinity, is the same. In twenty or fifty years' time it will have become commonplace that persons who take care of children must experience love themselves and that their organism must know the orgastic sensation and convulsion before they can understand a small child. I am well aware how repugnant that must sound to some ears today, yet in everyday experience it remains true that the greatest danger to the development of the child is represented by orgastically impotent educators.

The so-called autism of the small child—his stillness, his pallor, his withdrawnness—is an artifact of upbringing, a product of our total social misery. Diarrhea, anemia, etc., will soon be placed in this category too—a statement that may sound farfetched but is not. If the intestinal function is vegetative in nature, which it is, then the faulty emotional, i.e., orgone-biophysical, development of the child must play a crucial role also in diarrhea, pallor, anemia, and so on. To speak of "social misery" is meaningless actually, for in the final analysis this social misery is itself the result of a world of stultified human animals, of a world in which there is always more than enough money for wars but never enough—not even a minimal fraction of what is spent on paying the costs of one day of war—to ensure the protection of life. This is true because stultified, stiffened human beings have no understanding of what is alive; in fact, they fear it. There is no kind of social misery to equal the misery of the infants of biopathic parents.

It is a widespread misconception that grasping, crawling, walking, and similar functions are one day simply there, that a child just starts in grasping at the age of x weeks, crawling at the age of y weeks, and walking at the age of

z weeks. It is surprising that pediatricians have not worked out a schedule of how many steps an infant must take per day, just as they have determined the daily number of calories he should consume. A nipple that is erogenously alive, and warm contact with the mother, are much more effective than any chemical prescriptions in stimulating digestion and the total body functioning of the newborn. Once the contact is established between the infant and a warm, understanding environment, then—and only then— can natural processes be observed, rather than the artificial products of a pathological education. The educators themselves have to become sexually healthy before their scientific statements about children can be accurate. In my opinion, any statement should be, and no doubt one day will be, judged *according to the character structure of the person making it,* just as a book is judged by its stylistic elegance or a surgeon is judged by the dexterity of his hands.

A framework for accurate observations must first be established. If orgonotic contact is present, it is possible to see the various functions manifest themselves in the infant long before they have a "purpose." The eye, for instance, follows a moving hand. The closing motion of the hand develops long before the infant actually takes hold of any object and has nothing to do with mechanical "grasping reflexes." *Purposeful grasping develops gradually through the merger of many functions, i.e., through the contactful coordination of movements of previously uncoordinated organs.* Purposeful seeing, for instance, is established when the eye comes into contact with a pleasure-inducing movement in the surroundings. Once the act of seeing is accomplished, then the function, already complicated, seeks new pleasurable subjects on which to fix the gaze. Unpleasurable stimuli produce contraction and do not develop an act of seeing. The excessive amount of anxiety and displeasure experienced by our infants leads later to "dull eyes," "myopia," restriction of movement of the lids, and, with it, to the "dead" expression in the eyes.

In the face of these facts, what can be done with the mechanistic misconception that "seeing is the response of the retina to a light ray"? Certainly it is, but the reaction of the retina is only a vehicle, a means of seeing. *Is a child's dancing "only" the contact of feet and floor or "only" such and such a sequence of muscle contractions?* The emptiness of all the mechanistic interpretations of life is revealed here very clearly.

The child looks at you in one way when you smile at him and in another when you frown. *The crucial element, therefore, is the motor expression of the plasma,* not the individual stimuli, reactions, muscle contractions, etc. The light ray striking the retina always involves the same process of fixed wave lengths. Yet the infant's eye can be shining or dull depending upon the *tissue turgor,* which is increased by pleasure and inhibited by anxiety.

A person who has established good contact with the infant can encourage its functions. Whenever I came nearby, the infant I was observing made walking motions while lying down, to indicate to me his desire to "walk." When he was three and a half months old, he would become ecstatic as I held him under the arms and let him put his feet rhythmically on the floor and move along. He looked continuously at the walls or ceiling to convince himself that there really was movement, i.e., that the objects were moving past him.

Small children go through a phase of development characterized by vigorous activity of the voice musculature. The joy the infant derives from loud noises (crying, shrieking, and forming a variety of sounds) is regarded by many parents as pathological aggressiveness. The children are accordingly admonished not to scream, to be "still," etc. The impulses of the voice apparatus are inhibited, its musculature becomes chronically contracted, and the child becomes quiet, "well-brought-up," and withdrawn. The effect of such mistreatment is soon manifested in eating disturbances, general apathy, pallor of the face, etc. Speech disturbances and retardation of speech development are presumably caused in this manner. In the adult we see the effects of such mistreatment in the form of spasms of the throat. The automatic constriction of the glottis and the deep throat musculature, with subsequent inhibition of the aggressive impulses of the head and neck, seems to be particularly characteristic. Clinical experience has taught us that small children must be allowed to "shout themselves out" when the shouting is inspired by pleasure. This might be disagreeable to some parents, but questions of education must be decided *exclusively in the interests of the child,* not in those of the adults.

I want to make it clear that I see the origin of the biopathic shrinking process in *the dependency of psychic and physical-chemical functions on the bioemotional activity of the organism at the beginning of its development.* Here, and only here, will the means for the prevention of this process be found, not in drugs or cultural theories of sublimation.

I have stressed the dependence of psychosomatic functions on the bioenergetic functions of plasmatic pulsation. *Lively pulsatory activity from the first moment of birth is the only conceivable preventive against chronic contraction and premature shrinking.*

Bioenergetic pulsation is a function completely dependent on the stimulation from and contact with the environment. The character structure of the parents forms a crucial part of this environment, particularly that of the mother, *who provides the environment from the moment the embryo is formed until the moment of birth.*

I should like now to discuss the few insights we possess into the *prenatal* development of the organism. They do not amount to a great deal and are not decisive. Much more will have to be learned before it is possible to open up the obscure problem of heredity. But the following notes— they are no more than that—are a beginning that can lead to further practical knowledge.

If the onset of a shrinking biopathy is to be placed at the embryonic stage of development, the next question will concern the effect on the embryo of the orgonity [bio-energetic state] of the maternal organism, especially the genital organs.

The contractions of a chicken embryo, which have been demonstrated on film, confirm the clonic-pulsatory nature of embryonic growth. *The vitality of an embryo is manifested in these contractions.* The bladder-like form itself shows that the typical bioenergetic functions of protoplasmic protrusion, which can best be studied in flowing amoebae, are operative here. It is necessary to assume that a freely contractile uterus provides a much more favorable environment for the embryo than a spastic and anorgonotic uterus. In a uterus that is orgonotically vigorous, the circulation of blood and body fluids is more complete, making the energy metabolism more efficient. In addition, *the maternal tissues' capacity for charge is transmitted to the embryo. This is, after all, a functional part of the uterine mucosa.*

It is, therefore, perfectly understandable why the children of orgastically potent women are so much livelier than the children of frigid, armored women—a contention that can easily be confirmed. So-called heredity of temperament is in large measure nothing more than the effect of the maternal tissue on the embryo. Seen in this way, a part of the problem of "heredity of character" can be grasped for the first time. Since emotional functions are determined by the orgonotic energy functions, it is understandable that character is initially only a question of the degree of energy activity. In other words, *temperament is an expression of the quantity of the pulsatory activity of the orgonotic body system.*

The "heredity factor" would thus be tangible in principle as a quantitative energy factor. It is only logical that a system rich in energy resigns less easily than an energy-impoverished system. A legitimate conclusion is that the energy level of an embryo is determined by the energy level of the maternal genital organs. Quantitatively, energy deficiency can be understood as a decrease of orgonity, and it can be understood functionally as reduced pulsatory activity of the plasma. It is quite likely that the reduction of plasmatic pulsation in the embryo can secondarily cause an anorgonia. Thus, we cannot automatically assume that the embryo itself was initially anorgonotic, even though the mother may have suffered from decreased orgone energy metabolism. Two possibilities have to be considered: the internal anorgonia of the embryo, and the anorgonia resulting from that of the maternal genital apparatus.

Let us pursue this train of thought a little further. Naturally, concrete observations will correct or amplify what is obscure here.

During the sexual act of the parents, the embryo participates in the orgastic contractions of the uterus. It cannot be otherwise because of the physiological-anatomical situation. There are also developmental contractions in the embryo that cannot be distinguished bioenergetically from the contractions stimulated by the mother's orgasm. After birth, the newborn infant experiences independent orgastic contractions, at first principally in the head and neck region. If the female organism has possessed high orgonity before pregnancy, then the bioenergetic conditions for the orgonity of the embryo are favorable. These conditions are qualified postnatally by the genital structure of the parents, which continues in the realm of psychic development what the bioenergetic function established in the embryo.

Since high orgonity leads to strong, expansive, instinctual activity, anorgonia is prevented. The *anlage* of a carcinomatous shrinking biopathy or an anorgonia has thus become unlikely, though not entirely impossible. Destructive influences in later life can force even the most vigorous organism into resignation and shrinking.

But let us return to our newborn infant: From the fifth month of pregnancy on, the movements of the child were extraordinarily vigorous, so vigorous in fact that the mother often experienced pain. The obstetrician noticed that the child's heartbeat also was unusually strong. The delivery was a difficult one—a first pregnancy with premature rupture of the membranes and twenty hours' labor. Nevertheless, there was no asphyxia at birth. The mother's blood remained orgonotically strong and free of T-bacilli* throughout the entire pregnancy.

To recapitulate: *The biosocial prerequisites for strong orgonity of the child in utero are high orgonity and orgastic potency in the parents, absence of anorgonia in the uterus, and an absence of T-bacilli and no excess CO_2 in the maternal blood.*

Conversely, low orgonity and orgastic impotence in the parents, anorgonia of the uterus, disturbances of inner tissue

---

* T-bacilli are microscopically observable bodies which develop from the degeneration and putrid disintegration of living and non-living protein. See *The Cancer Biopathy.*

respiration, T-bacilli in the maternal blood, hyporgonia of the blood, and muscular armoring together create the disturbances of functioning now recognized as the possible cause of a later anorgonia in the child.

The mechanistic-mystical theory of heredity has thus lost more ground to functional pathology. The problem is no longer one of uncontrollable "inherited embryonic damage predisposing" the child to "hereditary cancer." Instead, we are dealing with changeable life functions, with energy quantities, and disturbances of pulsation. These disturbances do indeed create a tendency toward anorgonia, but the tendency does not have to develop if favorable circumstances eradicate the initial damage. The living organism is very adaptable to both the bad and the good conditions of life.

The time from the formation of the embryo to about the end of the first year of life is considered in orgone biophysics to be the critical period in which the "constitution of the orgonotic system of functioning" is established. This constitution, measured in terms of orgonity and the pulsatory capability of the tissues, determines the degree of plasmatic impulse activity.

Embryonic development should be thought of as terminating not at birth but at the time (around the age of ten to twelve months) when all the biological functions become fused into a unified, coordinated biosystem. This span of time is decisive for later bioenergetic functioning. The critical period for psychic development lies approximately in the third to fifth year of life. Its outcome is profoundly influenced by the progress of the earlier biophysical period. It is this earlier period that holds the solution to the puzzling fact that after treatment, even when all the pathological mechanisms have been worked through, an intangible *something* always remains—an undeviating hopelessness in the life activity, a stillness in the organism, an irritability—in brief, what classical psychiatry usually calls "inborn disposition."

Much remains obscure about the falling anxiety and anorgonia. Neither anxiety nor anger is a pathological manifestation of the life system. It is natural for a child to feel fear when it falls or is attacked by a dog, and it is natural for a newborn infant to express anger when its needs are not gratified. But falling anxiety is more than a fear of danger. It can appear long before there is any consciousness of danger. It is connected with rapid contractions of the vital apparatus, and, in fact, is produced by such contractions. Just as actual falling causes biological contraction, so contraction causes the sensation of falling. It is therefore understandable why a contraction that occurs in the process of orgastic *expansion* precipitates falling anxiety. And it is equally understandable why falling anxiety appears when the muscular armoring is pierced and the first plasmatic currents are felt. *A contraction occurring in the course of plasmatic expansion disturbs the sense of equilibrium.* But still something remains unexplained. Let us try to pinpoint it even if we are unable to explain it.

A basic function of the living orgonotic system is that it opposes and overcomes the earth's gravitational pull. The *dead* stalk of a leaf is completely subject to the force of gravity; the *living* stalk grows in a direction *opposite* to the force of gravity. (This phenomenon cannot, of course, be due simply to the processes of mechanical tension, since a dead stalk remains lying on the ground and does not raise itself even if filled with water.) The flight of birds depends on overcoming the force of gravity. The upright stance of man requires a vast amount of balance *against* the pull of gravity. We know that this balance fails when the unity of the body motor functions is somehow disturbed. This motor disturbance can be purely mechanical, such as a leg injury or tabes, but it can also be *functional*. Anorgonia of the entire body or of essential body organs signifies a disturbance of capacity for balance, hence a tendency to fall and the corresponding falling anxiety. The process is clear so far. But the manifestation of falling anxiety in a three-week-old infant (which we now know was precipitated by the cooling of the skin after a bath) remains mysterious. It is true that the function of rapid vascular contraction already exists, but the *experience* of falling does not. Where, then, does the *expression* of falling anxiety originate? Turning to a "phylogenetic experience" would explain nothing, because a phylogenetic experience is relevant only when anchored in actuality. Memory function does not exist without an actual mechanism.

At this point, we must give up trying to completely understand anorgonia and the falling anxiety and be content with understanding the connection between the blocking of orgonotic pulsation and the loss of organ sensation and equilibrium. The relation of orgonity and anorgonia to the force of gravity is clear. In the anorgonotic state the limbs are "heavy," and movement can be accomplished only with great effort. In the state of high orgonity, on the other hand, one feels "light," "floating." Let us take such figures of speech literally and seriously. *In anorgonia, less biological energy is free and active. The inert mass of the organism becomes greater and thus heavier in relation to the active energy that has to move the body. In high orgonity, more bioenergy is free and active, and the mass of the organism becomes lighter in relation to it.* What we are dealing with is a genuine, *alterable* relationship between mass and energy in the biosystem.

It is not possible to go any further at the present time

without invoking the metaphysical construct that supposedly thinks, feels, acts, and reacts in the background of
living functions. This would lead nowhere. We therefore
prefer to wait for a more favorable opportunity to finally
solve what remains unexplained. For the present it is
enough to understand how early and in what orgonotic
functions the carcinomatous shrinking process and its anorgonia set in.

Maltreatment of Infants

Over a period of several weeks I observed a curious phenomenon in the streets of New York. Mothers were taking
their babies for walks in their carriages on bright sunny
days, but the infants were lying on their stomachs. They
strained to hold their heads up, yet they kept falling down
again on the pillows. The dorsal muscles were tense. Some
of these infants were crying, others groaned, and a third
group was uttering despairing noises because of the physical effort they had to make. When I first saw infants in this
position, I thought the mothers had placed their babies on
their stomachs purely by chance. However, when I noticed
more and more of this infant torture going on around me,
it became clear that what we had here was another of those
sporadic and at the same time endemic manias aimed at
correcting nature in a very modern way, using "all technical
and scientific means."

Little more than two decades ago physicians and mothers,
in the same way, fostered the superstition that the naturally
bent knees of the infant should be straightened by force.
It was common practice to wrap the child up completely,
like a mummy, thus holding its body rigid. The infants
screamed, cried, and were unhappy, but since they could
not talk, they could not tell the doctors and mothers that
the bent leg joints were completely natural and that they
felt comfortable precisely in this position, whereas stretch-
ing their legs caused them pain and misery. At that time
doctors and mothers were concerned that the children's legs

would remain bent if they were not artificially straightened. After decades of such maltreatment of the infant's body, which had unimaginably serious consequences for the emotional development of the child, it was finally discovered that children still learn to walk properly even if they are allowed to hold their legs in the way that suits them best.

Scarcely had this torture been abolished when a new form of cruelty began to devastate the world of the infant —backed by the highest scientific authorities. Famous pediatricians in Europe, who consistently denied the infantile pleasure function, suddenly decided that the infant's food intake should be "strictly scientifically" controlled. Infants were only permitted a certain number of meals at their mother's breast, not one minute sooner or later than at a precisely defined time and not one gram less or more than what was "prescribed by science." Again the infants protested against *this* particular torture with wails and screams, but also with more serious kinds of protest reaction, such as grave intestinal disturbances. But again they were unable to express themselves directly.

We have since struggled to abolish a third type of massacre of infants and children, namely, the tying of their hands to prevent them from touching their genitals and sucking their thumbs. This maltreatment lasted for centuries and created many generations of neurotic people. Its sole purpose was to satisfy the adults' need not to be reminded of the sucking and masturbation desires they had experienced in their own childhood. It took a Freud and two generations of analytically trained pedagogues to launch the fight against this torture. We are still a long way from being able to claim that the infant or small child is permitted to give free rein to its pleasure function.

And now we are witnessing a new and obviously extremely up-to-date form of massacre. Instead of being able to look up at the beautiful blue sky, and at trees and human faces, the infant sees nothing but a white pillow. Instead of allowing the infant to retain the natural concave curvature of the vertebral column, people are "concerned about the dorsal muscles," and they produce lordosis not at puberty, as in the past, but as early as in infancy. If one inquires into the motive for this torturing of infants, the answer given is that this position "helps strengthen the muscles of the neck and back." On the other hand, we would like to know why the very latest theory of child-rearing is so concerned with the neck and back muscles but ignores the muscles of the abdomen, pelvis, genitals, etc. Wouldn't it be better and more sensible to make use of the many good exercises available for babies to keep the muscles of the body in good shape instead of creating such premature lordosis? There is every reason to be extremely skeptical about this latest concern with "infants' welfare." The physical posture which the infants are forced to adopt so early in life is exactly the same as that we find in chronically fixed form in adults as stiffening of the neck, back, and sacral muscles, with the corresponding chronic diseases, such as rheumatism, lumbago, lordosis, and scoliosis. This is precisely the posture that functions in opposition to the orgasm reflex.* The sternest possible warnings should be given about such measures. In reality, they are determined by irrational motives and not by concern for the infant. We are in full agreement with many early-childhood specialists that such artificial and unnatural measures should be opposed. We believe that the generally adopted prone position that is forced on the infants has disastrous effects on their physical and emotional development. This measure exposes the infant to an intolerable, grave, and damaging

---

* See *The Function of the Orgasm*.

conflict. We ought to promote and not hinder the natural functions of the body. The good old physicians, with many years of experience, maintained that the first principle of the art of medicine was "not to cause harm" and only to intervene where nature itself was unable to cope with lesions. However, the supine position is just as natural for infants as are the bent hip and leg joints. It seems urgent to act immediately with clear and resolute medical and pedagogical propaganda to stop this latest solicitous concern with the natural development of infants. If, however, occasionally an infant feels more comfortable lying on its stomach, then it should be allowed to do so. But an end should immediately be put to the *dictatorial imposition* of the prone position; otherwise a new generation of a hitherto unknown type of neurotic will be created.

Concerning Childhood Masturbation*

With regard to masturbation in childhood we may easily differentiate between three groups among our adult patients:

1. Psychoneurotics who fully achieved the phallic stage of libido development. These individuals engaged in genital masturbation and then, due to the specific outcome of the individual's Oedipus complex, either repressed genital eroticism to succumb later to hysteria or withdrew their libido from the genital position, regressing to earlier phases, and consequently succumbing to a compulsion neurosis or some other similar illness.†

2. Psychoneurotics who achieved the genital phase of libido development only incompletely or not at all, whether as a result of a powerful pregenital disposition (anal in particular) or because a severe castration trauma hindered them from proceeding to the genital libido stage. In these cases a process commenced which I have described as a "pregenital eroticizing of the genitals" and which is specific for a certain illness, namely, chronic hypochondriacal neu-

* Based on a discussion at the Vienna Psychoanalytic Association on November 2, 1927.

† Cf. Sigmund Freud, *The Disposition to Compulsion Neurosis*. Collected Works, Vol. V.

rasthenia.* In these patients we see that the genitals are cathected by pregenital wishes and fantasies. The genitals come to signify the breasts, the anus, or some other erogenous part of the body, while forgoing their own importance. This usually results in the most severe form of impotence, premature ejaculation while the penis is flaccid. Here, as Abraham first described, the glans penis has not become the primary zone and thus masturbation is altogether lacking.

3. Finally, among the few healthy individuals we have occasion to analyze, we observe that childhood masturbation was practiced undisturbed for a long period and that it re-emerged in puberty despite all guilt feelings.

If, additionally, we consider the occurrence of genital masturbation during childhood to be a favorable indication for prognosis and its absence (as in ejaculatio praecox, for example) an unfavorable one, we are constrained to conclude not only that infantile masturbation is not a sign of abnormality but, on the contrary, that it is the prerequisite for later genital primacy and a stable sexual life, as well as for mental health. Not only the prognostic significance of infantile masturbation but also the important role played by genital masturbation in the healing process teaches us that the ability (not the compulsion) to masturbate undistracted, without guilt or in the face of guilt, also belongs to mental health.

The issue here is not the injuriousness of infantile masturbation; on the contrary, it is the question of the inhibiting effects of upbringing. For this we must first clarify the nature of infantile masturbation. When speaking of genital masturbation in boys we are not referring solely to manipu-

---

* "On Chronic Hypochondriac Neurasthenia," in *Internationale Zeitschrift für Psychoanalyse*, Vol. XII (1926).

lation of the genitals but also to the essential genital fantasy, i.e., the desire to penetrate something with the penis (a cavity, etc.). This strikes a sadistic note in the desire as well as in the entire genital motor impulse.* As opposites to, or deviations from, this norm, we must cite all fantasies which may not be viewed as models for later intercourse. In girls, the situation is somewhat more complicated, as they normally do not masturbate vaginally but rather with the clitoris, the organ analogous to the penis.† However, in very favorable cases this active-phallic manipulation is coupled with a feminine fantasy such as submitting to the father. No matter how obscure such ideas may still be in young girls, their existence as a typical transitory phase is verifiable through depth analysis. Only during puberty does this fantasy attach itself to the vaginal zone, to the extent that other development proceeds normally.‡

The nature of the orgasm achieved is also important for an evaluation of infantile masturbation. In babies, masturbation occurs as mere local stimulation (supposedly), without fantasies. During puberty, fantasies and friction are augmented by ejaculation in boys and a similar process in

---

* *1949:* The above statement about the sadistic coloration of the boy's genitality is, of course, wrong. It was made years ago under the influence of the erroneous psychoanalytic concept that all male genitality had a sadistic quality.

† *1949:* The statement that the girl's clitoral masturbation is normal is also due to the then prevalent psychoanalytic concept that the little girl had no vaginal genitality. The lack of vaginal genitality was later shown by sex-economy to be an artifact of our culture, which suppresses genitality completely and instills castration anxiety not only in the boy but also in the girl. This creates a true secondary drive in the form of penis envy and predominance of clitoral genitality. Psychoanalytic theory mistook these artificial secondary drives for primary, natural functions.

‡ However, we feel that drawing little girls' attention to their vaginas might be indicated.

girls. In childhood, however, genital fantasies are present, but the orgasm follows the course of a shallow curve, ascending and descending with no distinct climax. The sensations experienced in infantile masturbation might be best compared to scratching an intense itch.

The circumstances under which the child experienced the first masturbational sensations in the genitals are especially important. Frequently the fate of the later sexual constitution depends upon this. Thus, genital excitation first experienced during a beating may fixate masochism; excitation during urination may result in a preponderance of urethral pleasure and bed-wetting if a strict upbringing is also a contributing factor. Very often genital excitation arises in connection with fear, for example, when parental copulation is overheard and interpreted as a sadistic act. This *"Angstlust"* leads to a fixation of anxious expectations whenever any genital sensation arises. It then becomes markedly pronounced in puberty, when it is augmented by the orgasm, which is experienced as a frightening, overwhelming sensation robbing one of clear consciousness. Some cases of protracted or avoided end-pleasure may be traced to infantile fear of sexual excitation. In any case, however, all of these experiences harm the normal genital function in a more or less pronounced way and hence also establish a disposition to neurosis.

Spite toward an inhibiting upbringing, *Angstlust,* and a considerable amount of hate toward the denying object are usually the main causes for the fixation of childhood masturbation. One must assume that just as somatic development of the genital apparatus engenders the libido functions at birth and during puberty, it is also a somatic genital thrust at the Oedipal age upon which genital organization and masturbation are based. This assumption is a psychoanalytic necessity, although its validation is the task of physiology.* The waning of this assumed somatic thrust and of the Oedipal phase itself should be accompanied by a decrease—or a total cessation—of masturbation; if this does not occur, a severely inhibiting upbringing alone may be blamed. Still, it is better that unenlightened education cause fixation of masturbation than that it be thwarted altogether once it has commenced, or even prevented from the start. The attempts of "progressive" parents to "gently distract" their children from masturbation must be evaluated with caution, for children doubtless possess an unerring sense of the adult unconscious which is trying to prevent genital pleasure gains.

As far as can be determined, the only danger in masturbation lies in its prohibition. Without entirely thwarting masturbation, this creates guilt feelings and hypochondriacal anxiety, which disturbs the course of excitation during the act itself and causes neurasthenia. Freud's hypothesis that excessive masturbation causes neurasthenia is correct, as I have attempted to demonstrate with copious material in another context, with the qualification that the disturbance is directly related to the influence of guilt feelings in the course of excitation. Individuals who masturbate without such direct dispersion of excitation do not develop neurasthenia, although a psychoneurosis will arise if masturbation is not replaced, in due time, by sexual satisfaction through intercourse.

* *1949:* This assumption has been proven true through the discovery of the organismic orgone energy which governs the sexual apparatus. It clearly shows three peaks in functioning during the first twenty years of life. The first is a surging of sexuality shortly after birth, the second around the fifth year of life, and the third through several years of puberty. Thus, the physiological assumption of early psychoanalysis about the development of infantile genitality has been confirmed as well as put on a sound bioenergetic foundation.

The lack of adequate practical data prohibits our discussing the possible dangers of complete nonrestriction of infantile as well as pubertal masturbation. Those who incline to be pessimistic in this regard, or are apprehensive about cultural sublimation, must be reminded that satisfied genitality rarely hinders sublimation, whereas unsatisfying sexual activity shattered by guilt feelings always does. Moreover, future experience in this field will probably demonstrate how greatly even analyzed adults are burdened with sexual repression. It is this repression which, in questions pertaining to masturbation and sexuality in general, prohibits the formulation of a simple concept corresponding to natural functions.

A Conversation with a Sensible Mother

MOTHER: In the last issue of the *Journal of Political Psychology and Sex-Economy* I was reading the article on the sexual enlightenment of a three-year-old girl. When one reads it, everything seems perfectly clear and so simple. But things are not that simple, after all.

REICH: If I remember correctly, there is no mention in the article that it is such a simple matter. Do tell me though what reservations you have. I know that in other respects you have a very sensible approach to the sexual enlightenment of children.

MOTHER: To be honest, I must admit that many years ago my views were essentially the same as those expressed in the article, but the negative and disappointing experiences I have had with my own children forced me to change my mind.

REICH: Please elaborate.

MOTHER: As you know, when my daughter, who is now fifteen, was only three or four years old, I educated her absolutely correctly about sexual matters. But now I find that she has turned into a difficult child and that what I told her has not helped her at all.

REICH: If I understand you correctly, you expected at the time that by giving your daughter a fully consistent sexual education she would not turn into a difficult child. What are the problems, then?

146

MOTHER: Well, for example, she is terribly afraid of masturbating. How can one explain this? We not only fully explained the differences between the sexes to her when she was still very young, but we also stressed that she should feel free to masturbate if she wanted to and that people who forbid this or regard it as bad are in the wrong. I would even say that we overdid it, because my husband and I used to bathe together in the nude, and we also discussed these matters very frankly. If the child now displays such obvious genital timidity, the only possible conclusion is that sexual enlightenment has not worked in her case.

REICH: The way you describe it, the situation really does appear strange and seems in fact to run counter to the views of those who support the consistent sexual education of children. What would you do today in the light of your experience?

MOTHER: I can't say. I'm not certain anymore. I would probably tell her less than we did at the time and not force it on her.

REICH: So you think that the lack of success is due to too much sexual education. But look here, so far we have taken it for granted that the child has not turned out well. However, that is really a relative concept. What do you actually have to complain about?

MOTHER: My daughter is not as even-tempered as I would like her to be. She has frequent outbursts of rage, which bother her; she is often grumpy and dissatisfied with school and life around her; she goes through periods of boredom—in short, there is something wrong.

REICH: Have you tried psychoanalysis?

MOTHER: Yes, she has been seeing a psychoanalyst for almost three years, but it seems to me that although she has become somewhat calmer and more composed, basically nothing has changed.

REICH: Let us try to break the problem down in order to understand it. The phenomena about which you complain are not all in the same category, nor do they have the same origin or importance. Let us consider school, for example. You say the child is dissatisfied with school. How is she doing academically?

MOTHER: Extremely well. Everyone agrees that her intelligence and skills are well above average. But she does not enjoy school.

REICH: Has it always been like that?

MOTHER: No, there were times when she liked going to school.

REICH: Can you describe any external circumstances which may have caused the change?

MOTHER (*thinks for a moment*): I am not sure if it is true, but now that I think of it, she has always been dissatisfied whenever she attended public, state-run schools. For example, for a time she attended a Montessori-type school, where she got on very well.

REICH: Do you think perhaps that there are genuine reasons for being dissatisfied with school—perhaps the teaching methods put off such an intelligent child.

MOTHER: That is quite possible. But how can she get by and manage in life if this is so?

REICH: Look, we have now uncovered a contradiction which you don't seem to understand fully. I think you equate a peaceful and balanced disposition with a healthy state, and a tendency toward agitation and protest with being neurotic and a failure. I think we can quickly agree that compared with a lively, intelligent, and critical child, an inhibited, neurotic child will react less intensely to objectively unfavorable teaching methods that are not suited to children's needs.

MOTHER: Yes, I think I could go along with that. But

what has that got to do with her inhibition regarding masturbation? Her [female] psychoanalyst and I both share the view that a child should possess a genital structure and should not be afraid of masturbation. I know that one should not force her to do it if she does not want to, but in her case I cannot explain her fear, because we explicitly permitted her to masturbate.

REICH: Wait a moment. You just used the word "permitted." But we can really only permit something that is otherwise forbidden, and we both know that in general children are forbidden to masturbate. However, I suggest that we examine two questions that need to be answered before we can understand the matter:

1. What sort of sexual life does your child have?

2. How did you raise your child until the time you told her everything about sex?

Let us start with the first question: Does the child have what one could call a sex life?

MOTHER (*somewhat surprised*): What do you mean by that?

REICH: Well, I mean literally. Does the child engage in any kind of sexual activity? Does she experience sexual gratification?

MOTHER (*somewhat agitated*): I don't understand you, Doctor. I was just complaining that she is afraid of masturbating and does not allow herself any genital sexual activity, although we have nothing against it.

REICH: Just listen to me patiently for a minute. It is not only what you allow the child that matters. You must also consider the other circumstances in her life. What sort of life does the child lead?

MOTHER: When I was working abroad, she lived for a long time in a home; now she is living with me.

REICH: And what were things like in the home?

MOTHER: Oh, she had a brief flirtation with a boy, but it was nothing serious.

REICH (*astonished*): Now look here, why do you immediately call this love affair a harmless flirtation and nothing serious? How do you arrive at that conclusion?

MOTHER: It can't have been anything serious, because she was, after all, suffering from genital anxiety.

REICH: I believe that this is another mistake on your part. Because the child suffers from genital anxiety, that is to say, is afraid to have a genital relationship with a boy, you conclude that this flirtation must have been harmless. Don't you think it possible that this flirtation was a very serious matter, indeed, as serious as any love affair is for a child, and that the child pretended the matter was harmless because she was unable to see the affair through and yet she had to deal with it somehow, e.g., by playing it down.

MOTHER: I have often discussed this question with my husband; he feels that I underestimated the whole affair, because apparently she talked it over very seriously with him. I don't believe this, however, because the child knows that her father would like her to be genitally healthy, and she tells him what he wants to hear.

REICH: All right, let us assume for a moment that this is the case. Does this prove that her falling in love was not serious? I can't see that.

MOTHER (*somewhat confused*): Yes, but after all, she suffers from genital anxiety.

REICH: There we are, we are back to square one again. You have to admit—particularly because you are in all other respects so sensible in your relationship with your child, unlike most mothers—that your daughter finds herself in a dilemma. At root her genital desires are genuine and they are expressed in a genuine way; however, when it comes to actual activity, they are diverted into something "harmless" or into anxiety. You should be able to see that. You should not treat the child's love affair as trivial, just because she is troubled by genital anxiety. On the contrary, precisely because the child comes up against the barriers of anxiety, she feels all the more confused by her own drives. And aren't you forgetting that you are not dealing with a child that is unaware of her own sexuality? After all, she knows everything, discusses everything—isn't that so?

MOTHER: Yes, I know that she thinks and talks a lot about such things, but I avoid discussing them with her, because I do not wish to force her into something that she is not yet mature enough to handle.

REICH: Now we understand each other better. If a child knows everything and, because it has been educated sexually, regards genital sexuality as something natural and straightforward, then it follows clearly that the child does not find it easier but instead much more difficult than other children to cope with genital fears. In such cases, genital anxiety plays quite a different role than in a child having a negative genital structure. Can you tell me how the psychoanalyst is handling this question?

MOTHER: Well, she is doing what is customary in such cases. My daughter is being made aware of her fear of her own genital drives.

REICH: Is that all she is doing?

MOTHER: What else can any analyst do?

REICH: Here we have another place where a mother is uncertain and a child is made unhappy. Do you think that a living, active function can be handled satisfactorily merely by *talking* about it? Although talking is a first step toward change, one cannot leave it at that. The anxiety that a child experiences psychically is rooted in a certain course of development of its genital functions, and we know from experience that genital disturbances in adults, for example, should not be treated in a vacuum but must be altered in a very concrete way. This is done as follows: The morbid mode of genital activity, which is certainly present, is not accepted as an expression of their natural genital drives, and therefore they are not encouraged to indulge in this morbid activity free of anxiety and feelings of guilt. The right approach is quite different. Once the genital anxiety in particular has become rooted in aberrant muscular actions, the actions, movements, and physical behavior of the child must be unmasked as a device which protects her from genuine orgastic genital activity. I base this statement on my experience with adults and children. I am quite certain that this is the case with your child as well.

MOTHER: Yes, I have heard of something like this, but I cannot understand that genital masturbation acts as a protection against genital masturbation. And the anxiety is not really supposed to be linked with masturbation, but instead the pathological form of masturbation is supposed to be a means by which anxiety prevents the biological genital rhythm from surfacing. I do not understand this.

REICH: It is not easy to understand, and yet it is quite simple. You see, from childhood on, once their biological and natural rhythms have been destroyed by education, most people develop another means, an artificial form, of genital activity—if they do not abandon such activity altogether. It has recently become known that most analysts commit the serious error of regarding the actions that replace biological and natural genitality as *true* genitality, whereas in fact they serve a defensive function. Do you see that?

MOTHER: Yes, I can understand that, because I have

read a lot about it. But I cannot imagine it in practical terms.

REICH: There is a sure symptom by which this can be detected. If one allows a person with this kind of inhibition to relax fully for a while, as far as he or she can, then without doing anything at all, spontaneous waves of vegetative excitation occur, particularly in the genital region. At the same time, when genital anxiety exists, restlessness will occur; this is not an expression of excitation but, as exact studies have shown, the purpose of these actions is to quell the excitation. As far as I know, psychoanalysts do not acknowledge this fact. An analysis of genital inhibitions can then be pursued ad infinitum, but it will never meet with success because it is based on false premises.

MOTHER: Yes, now I understand something about it; but how is it possible that my child can be so afraid of excitation? She was sexually enlightened, after all.

REICH: I will try to explain what we are dealing with here by means of a simple example. Assume a child was physically active and lively up until age three or four and romped around like a child should. It climbed on tables and benches, slid down banisters; in short, it behaved like a young wild animal. Unlike many, we of course do not regard this as unnatural or annoying—on the contrary. Now imagine that this child is then told that romping around, running, and jumping are absolutely natural and normal, that they are good things to do, and that anybody who said they were bad is wrong. The child would now want to romp about. But let us assume that it has no opportunity to do so and instead must sit still for one reason or another; let us take the example one step further and assume that the child had to remain still for years and could not move or use its body in the way nature intended. By the time the child turned fifteen, it would not only be paralyzed, but more than that: if you tried to get the child to move its muscles again, it would certainly develop anxiety at such an idea.

You are guilty of the same error that so many progressive pedagogues, including those of the Freudian school, commit. On the one hand, you approve of sexual education and you do not deny, at least not theoretically, the possibility of romping around, i.e., in our case the child's true sex life. However, you judge the final result not on the basis of the child's *actual* life, as it evolves in accordance with external and internal conditions, but only on the basis of whether and how she has been sexually educated. It should not be difficult for you to comprehend that a child that has not been sexually enlightened and does not indulge in any sexual activity is much better off than a child that has been enlightened but actually behaves as if it had not been. This is the first point.

MOTHER: All right, I understand that. But we never prevented our child from being sexually active.

REICH: Theoretically not; but in practice you did. Please be patient a little while longer. What is at stake here is something very important and decisive for the child. Did you regard the burgeoning love affair with the young boy as harmless? In so doing, did you not shirk your responsibility to give the child further guidance, since you ought to have known that the child needed support in this conflict? You did not even discuss the matter with the child.

MOTHER: Are you telling me that I should force myself on her? I give her complete freedom of action; she can do what she likes. I do not stop her.

REICH: There you are, you see, once again you are wrong. We agreed that the general environment in which the child lives makes it impossible for her to be sexually active.

Is this environment as neutral as you are? No, it isn't. The environment hinders the child in every way imaginable, through atmosphere, through direct influence, through school, etc. Thanks to its sexual education, the child has relatively uninhibited genital demands, but in fact it faces a world hostile to sexuality; and in this situation you take the stance of allowing the child to do what it wants. You make no distinction between forcing a child to do something it does not want and supporting a child in something which it does want but which causes it a certain kind of anxiety. This is the social side of the matter.

MOTHER: I have to think all that over first. It is too much to take in all at once. I still cannot quite understand why the child cannot find her own way to do something for which we have granted all the necessary freedom.

REICH: Yes, this is precisely the point on which the second question hinges. Not only must the child battle with the entire world; worse still, its fighting spirit is weakened by its fear of organ-pleasure—we have already established that. Shall we now examine this question?

MOTHER: I still do not understand why you think that is such a problem. She is simply suffering from genital anxiety and is therefore afraid to become genitally active.

REICH: I see that if you do not consider the second question, the whole thing remains unclear to you. The anxiety which assails the child from outside must somehow have taken root in the child in order to have an effect —do you agree?

MOTHER: Yes, I fully understand that.

REICH: You claim, and let us assume you are right in doing so, that neither you nor your husband has instilled genital anxiety in the child. Let us assume, therefore, that the difference between this child and other children is that although she exhibits genital anxiety, she did not acquire this anxiety from outside during childhood. There are only two possibilities left: either the general social climate has had this effect on the child, or, if we eliminate that, the only other possibility is that there is yet another reason for this genital anxiety having taken root. Where should we look for it?

MOTHER: I don't understand.

REICH: Let us try to guess a little bit. A child's development in the period of genital excitation is not determined solely by experiences during that period but also, and in particular, by earlier experiences. Can you perhaps remember how you toilet-trained the child?

MOTHER (*silent for a moment*): I don't know whether I am supposed to have a guilty conscience here.

REICH: Oh, please, we are not concerned at this point with whether your conscience is clear or not; we are trying to clarify a situation that is unfortunate for the child.

MOTHER: Yes, I have to admit that in the first two years of her life neither my husband nor I understood clearly what we were doing. Right up until her third birthday, possibly even longer, she suffered from the habit of soiling her bed.

REICH: Did you say "suffered"? Why "suffered"? It is quite natural that up to that age, and perhaps beyond, a child occasionally soils its bed. Did it happen often?

MOTHER: No, not too often; only for a certain period of time, lasting several weeks, when she wet her bed each night and occasionally soiled herself.

REICH: What did you do about it?

MOTHER: We always scolded her and pointed out that she had done wrong; I remember that we did this even before she had learned to talk, when she was about one year old.

REICH: Can you perhaps remember any special changes which took place in the child?

MOTHER: I know that she had a bad spell of screaming and defiance between the ages of two and three and that she occasionally had terrible screaming fits and could not be calmed down.

REICH: Now things are falling into place at last. As you know, a child always reacts with fits of screaming and defiance when the people responsible for its upbringing forbid it to do something or do so at a time when the child cannot understand the why or the wherefore. This is perhaps one of the most tragic experiences that a child can have. It does something quite harmless without realizing it has done something "bad." The parents, just as blindly, fear for the child's "cultural" future and let fly indiscriminately.

MOTHER: Yes, I know that. I understand that now. But what has this got to do with genital anxiety? That is what we are talking about.

REICH: It has a great deal to do with it. You see, according to psychoanalytic theory, the retention of feces is a source of pleasure to the infant. Recent research has shown that this explanation is incorrect. The process is as follows: Initially, the child experiences its anal function as something completely harmless and derives only the appropriate pleasure from it. Then, usually at a very early age, perhaps even at six months—at the latest, however, at the age of one—a more or less strict ban is placed on soiling the bed. Now, the child *experiences anxiety in releasing its feces,* not, as psychoanalysts claim, pleasure in retaining it. Naturally, this expresses itself objectively as retention and it looks as if the child was continuing to experience its former pleasure in another form. However, this is not so. To start with, the child is afraid of the consequences of releasing its feces. When does it begin to retain them? When it experiences the familiar feeling—the urge to defecate—in the bowel. If you think about it, you will find that the sensations one has at such a time are very similar to those experienced when the genitals are aroused. Thus as soon as the bowel sensation is experienced, the child tenses up, full of anxiety, and retains its feces. This is how the various forms of infantile constipation originate.

MOTHER: Yes, but I still don't understand it.

REICH: But you soon will. The child faces a conflict between an inner tension and a fear that prevents the inner tension from being released. If the bowel is evacuated during sleep, and if the disciplinary measures are repeated, then the conflict in the child is intensified. Analyses have shown clearly that the so-called defiance displayed by the child at this early age always occurs when toilet-training is carried out approximately in the manner described above. Two distinct phases can be recognized. In the first phase of the defiance reaction the child resists the violation perpetrated on it by its educators—but this is still a healthy reaction. Then, under the pressure of guilt feelings or of fear of losing the affection of its educator, the defiance emerges and becomes compulsive and self-torturing. This is what your child has gone through.

MOTHER: Yes, but I still don't understand what this has to do with genital anxiety.

REICH: You will. When a child marked by such experiences from the period of toilet-training enters the genital phase, it will automatically find itself in the situation your child is in now. Although it has freely, intellectually and emotionally, accepted genital activity as such, this activity is naturally linked with certain sensations of current in the genitals. If the child has undergone toilet-training of the kind you have described, and even if she does not connect the activities, she does connect the bowel sensations, which she learned to associate with danger, with the genital sensations, which are qualitatively the same. The child then develops genital anxiety, which affects the genitals. In reality, however, it is fear of defecating and not genital anxiety as such that is involved.

MOTHER: Now I am finally beginning to understand.

REICH: You and your daughter will be all the better for it.

MOTHER: Yes, but there is one thing that I do not understand. My daughter is undergoing psychoanalysis; will that solve her anal inhibitions as well?

REICH: That is another mistake which dominates modern analytic therapy. The aim should not be to recognize and "interpret" a fear as such; instead, it is important to develop the only method that is adequate to reverse the shift that anxiety or its underlying sensations of current have made from the anus to the genitals. This cannot be done simply through interpretation nor, as experience has shown, can it be achieved through simple resistance analysis. A technique is required which breaks down in a certain sequence the various forms of defense which the child has built up. However, I cannot say any more about it now. Unfortunately, this is too technical for the untrained lay person to understand.

MOTHER: But what should I do now?

REICH: To start with, you should let today's discussion sink in; check what we have said against your child's day-to-day life; become clear in your own mind whether deep down, in your own inner attitude toward things, you are ready to put into practice what you accept intellectually. Very often it is their own former experiences that prevent mothers from practicing the conclusions drawn from their conviction and knowledge. I am sure we shall meet again. I hope that we will then understand each other even better than we do today. These are very difficult matters, and not all of them are yet known or understood. Everything takes time to mature.

The Sexual Rights
of Youth*

INTRODUCTION

The following pages were written for young people, without any upper or lower age limit. My purpose in setting down these remarks is not to provide the usual kinds of "sex education," which avoids the question of adolescent sexual intercourse; instead it is my intention, based on well-founded scientific conviction, to give young people a definite answer to the serious questions that they have about their maturing sexuality:

- What is involved in the process of sexual maturing?
- Why are sexual matters treated in such a secretive manner in school, at home, and by the public in general?
- What is the significance of the moodiness, states of excitation, compulsive daydreams, isolation, and sexual fears that occur at this age? and
- What is the way out of this situation?

The state of modern society, current developments at home and at school, and also the influence of public opinion in general make boys and girls eagerly snatch up books and writings on sex education. Ninety-nine times out of a hun-

* Written specifically for young people in the Sexpol movement and published in 1932 as *The Sexual Struggle of Youth*, this work was later revised by Reich, who made significant changes, including a new title.

dred the sort of books they get their hands on are rubbish, the poorly contrived efforts of unscrupulous profiteers or of sexually ignorant physicians who know how to exploit fully the great need for clarity that is experienced by young people from all walks of life. Young people are contaminated, on the one hand, by moralizers and advocates of abstinence and, on the other, by pornographic literature. Both influences are extremely dangerous, the former no less than the latter.

The sexual misery of modern youth is immeasurable. But most of it is out of sight, beneath the surface.

We will present facts to demonstrate that the dilemma facing young people is quite different from what it is generally believed to be. The choice is not between a moralistic and abstinent life on the one hand and sexual smut on the other, but between a healthy and a pathological sexual life. The fact is that all young people and children, *without exception,* indulge in sexual activity, even those who most loudly promote "sexual morality." For, in the final analysis, moral intimidation has the same effect as pornographic literature and as the conditions in which most of our young people grow up.

The central question is that of sexual intercourse in adolescence and the attitude of society toward it. Young people have more than merely a right to be "enlightened"; they are fully entitled to their emotional health and their sexual joy in life.

This right has been taken away from them. Countless young people have lost all awareness of their sexuality, although this has opened the way to serious psychic disturbances during puberty. Therefore, we will not give advice "from on high," nor will we seek to "educate"; instead, we will try to give a full and undistorted presentation of the true facts, to teach young people to understand the situation in which they find themselves and to show them that they must take matters into their own hands if they seriously wish to put an end to this misery. One does not beg for a right, one fights for it.

This applies to those people who in a woolly, fuzzy manner follow the preachings of the moralizers and ruin themselves in the process. There are many boys and girls who will find that the questions dealt with here are self-evident or who will not have much difficulty in understanding them. On the other hand, there are many who will have some problems in absorbing the contents of the following pages. And again, there are others in the same age group who have been so badly led astray by compulsory morality and education that they will at first reject what is said because it embarrasses or enrages them. Many a young person approaching puberty must develop a moralistic, defensive attitude against the unconscious urges of his sexuality, as well as against any knowledge from outside, simply in order to give himself an artificial prop to cling to. He is unaware of the relationship between his sexuality and the daydreams that torture him, his moodiness, his states of excitation, and other plights; he acts and thinks under the compulsive authority of a foreign will that forbids him to obtain sexual knowledge. This foreign will stems from education and has become a part of his own character, which now acts contrary to his natural bodily needs. We must understand very clearly that the question of adolescents and sex is not just a difficult one but may in many cases prove to be explosive.

However, this should not intimidate us. There is no other way. We must decide: either we go on facing psychic misery, suffering, suicide, and pregnancies without end, or we choose the truth, which under present conditions may appear harsh but does offer the prospect of a definitive solution.

The decision about the sexual rights of young people must be taken by the young people themselves.

SEXUAL TENSION AND GRATIFICATION

The usual approach to the problem of educating young people in sexual matters is to start and finish with the "mystery of propagation." However, we know and wish to state clearly what everyone else knows but dares not put into words, namely, that in reality the main problem causing young people so many headaches is how to cope with sexual excitation and the forbidden pleasure of gratifying sexual desires. We also know that it is precisely this point, this aspect of the sexual problem, around which the tender-hearted "educators" so gingerly skirt.

Only rarely do a man and a woman engage in sexual intercourse with the express intention of having a child. However, the Church, the school system, and science would all like to make us believe that the only purpose of the sexual act is to produce children. If this were so, then the human race would long ago have died out within two or three generations and certainly would not have survived the present economic misery of the masses. In reality, people have sexual intercourse because they are driven to do so by sexual tension and because of the sexual gratification that accompanies it. Sexual gratification guarantees propagation of the species because impregnation is linked with the sex act. The Church always cites "nature" when it asserts that intercourse for any purpose other than pro-

creation is "unnatural." Strangely enough, nature has committed a major error by creating a sexual apparatus that
does not merely encourage people to perform the sexual
act whenever they want to, or are able to have children;
instead, it has arranged things in such a way that the
healthy person on average experiences the desire for sexual intercourse about one to three times a week. In the
course of people's lives, therefore, they have intercourse
on several thousand occasions, but generally only on two
or three occasions is intercourse performed for the purpose
of creating a child. And it is even more strange, seen from
the standpoint of the Church or the narrow-minded citi-
zen, that throughout the animal kingdom, to which man
also belongs, procreation is associated with a high degree
of sexual pleasure, i.e., with precisely that element which
is most condemned and on which our young people have
probably been given the least amount of information. We
must say, therefore, that anyone who discusses the problem
of sex without mentioning the aspect of sexual pleasure is
being intentionally or unintentionally misleading. This is
not just an idle claim but can be backed up by proof.

We must distinguish between the following problems in
this area:

1. How does the sexual apparatus function naturally?

2. Do the institutions within which we live inhibit or
encourage sexual gratification?

3. If they inhibit gratification, why and for what purpose?

4. Is there any way of alleviating the sexual distress
suffered by young people?

5. If not, then under what circumstances can young
people achieve sexual liberation, and what must they do to
obtain this release?

Sexual maturity

The sexual tension or excitation with which every youth is familiar is the expression of a physical process through which the sexual apparatus—in the man, certain parts of the testicles, and in the woman, certain tissues in the ovaries—produces substances called hormones which enter the bloodstream and create a state of sexual arousal in the nervous system. While the testicles and ovaries are the most important organs for sexual excitation, they are not the only ones. Other internally secreting glands, such as the pituitary, are involved. Sexual excitation emanating from the sense organs, from eyes, skin, nose, ears, also have an important effect. In fact, there is not one part of the body which is not to some degree affected by sexual stimuli. The areas of the body that are particularly excitable are called the "erogenous zones." The physical state of sexual tension is manifested psychically as an urge to release the tension, i.e., to seek sexual gratification. It can be proved that for decades science has for moral reasons ignored the fact that these states of tension do not occur just at the time of puberty but appear and begin to have an effect in early childhood. It is just that during puberty the tensions become particularly intense because now the sexual apparatus is producing sperm or eggs and the entire body reaches full maturity.

The intensified functioning of the sexual apparatus goes together with heightened emotional sensitivity, which, given the conditions to which youth is subjected, almost always leads to tortured agitation, daydreaming, and excessive fantasizing. Puberty commences at different times in different people. On average, however, it occurs between the ages of twelve and fourteen. In boys, the voice starts to deepen, a heavy growth of hair develops in the pubic region, and quite frequently he experiences his first nocturnal emissions of semen. In girls, the breasts begin to swell and the monthly period commences. A state of general tension builds up in both sexes. This is the age during which the capacity for work tends to decline because the person's attention is drawn more and more toward sexual matters. The frequent erections experienced by the young man and the increased blood flow and tension in the sexual organs of the young woman indicate that these young people are now physically mature enough for sexual intercourse. Different people take different amounts of time to reach full maturity. In one person the process is over in a matter of weeks or months, while another takes years. Therefore, it is not possible to give a general answer to the question: When is a person ready for sexual intercourse? There is no law that applies to all.

The significantly increased level of sexual excitation seeks an outlet. This is the point where the sexual problems of young people commence, because they have only three choices: sexual intercourse, masturbation, or abstinence.

Masturbation by young people

Before a young person becomes mature enough for sexual intercourse, the sexual drive is operative in various forms from early childhood onward. One of them, which ultimately comes increasingly to the fore as a transitional stage in the development toward a mature sex life, is masturbation. The Church has always regarded masturbation by children and young people as a serious vice that is dangerous and potentially damaging to a person's health.*
It is only recently that modern sexology has condescended

* At this time, in 1983, masturbation is still considered a mortal sin by the Catholic Church.—*Eds.*

to recognize masturbation as an entirely normal transitional form of infantile and youthful sexuality. People have racked their brains to explain why young persons are driven to masturbate. Not until the belief that masturbation is a vice had been dropped did it become obvious that masturbation is simply the expression of physical and emotional sexual tension in the adolescent organism. In principle, it is no different from scratching or rubbing the skin to relieve an itch, because it, too, involves a state of tension in an organ, which can be eliminated by rubbing. Of course, masturbation differs from ordinary rubbing to relieve an itch in that the tension in the organ and the gratification felt at its release are much more intense.

There has also been a great deal of argument about whether masturbating is harmful or not. Some defend it as harmless while others just as unflaggingly insist that it is harmful. The question is wrongly put in this manner. What we have to ask is when and under what conditions masturbation is harmful or harmless. Until recently, abstinence was emphasized as the only possible path for young people to follow in life and the best way to avoid difficulties. Similarly, some people later went all the way in the other direction and committed the error not only of insisting that masturbation was utterly harmless but of advocating it as the only way out of and indeed the best solution to young people's problems. We shall see that this view merely skirts the most important and difficult issue of young people's sexual lives, namely, the question of sexual intercourse. Individual or mutual masturbation by children and adolescents before they attain sexual maturity is essentially the result of natural physical causes. At the time when sexual maturity has been reached, however, there are also social reasons why masturbation is the sole form of sexual activity available to young people, because sexual inter-

course at this age is made difficult or impossible by a
number of institutional measures. By the time a person
attains sexual maturity, masturbation is no longer a natural
form of sexual activity, as shown by the fact that among
primitive tribes which place no barrier in the way of young
people wishing to have intercourse, masturbation plays an
insignificant role.

In order to correctly assess masturbation we must distinguish between the disturbed and the normal forms of
this type of sexual activity. To judge what constitutes
healthy, harmless masturbation in the early stages of maturity, we must consider a young boy who discovers masturbation without being influenced by parents, Church, or
the scurrilous literature on the subject. The boy experiences
a feeling of tension in his sex organ; he touches it and
manipulates it, initially quite unconsciously. Often he
ejaculates, much to his surprise, and experiences a feeling
of sexual relief. Then a period of sexual inactivity sets in
for two to four days, until the sexual tension builds up
again. The boy is now familiar with the feeling of tension
and relaxation and masturbates deliberately. He does not
feel guilty, does not think that he is harming himself by
masturbating, and therefore does not interrupt the flow of
excitation. Such young people remain absolutely healthy
until the fear of God is put into them by some friend, by
parents, or by one of the usual trashy books which fall into
their hands. Now, for the first time, they begin to feel that
they are doing something terrible; for the first time they
start to resist the urge to masturbate. The process is exactly
the same, regardless of whether it takes place in a boy or a
girl. Either they try to suppress totally the desire to manip-
ulate their own sex organs or they permit themselves to
masturbate up to a certain point, but usually believe that
orgasm, which results in a slight clouding of consciousness

(and, also, in the girl causes copious moistening of the walls of the vagina), is particularly harmful. But this is exactly what they should not do; this is where the actual physical and psychic damage or, more correctly expressed, the damage arising from inhibition or blocking of the normal course of sexual excitation begins to develop. Because the sequence of excitation is interrupted, the nervous system is profoundly upset, and the symptoms about which young people complain are the expression of genuine physical damage. It is not the masturbation itself but the inhibition of masturbation and the attendant feelings of guilt, anxiety, and remorse that are the source of the harmful effects. Therefore, once masturbation has been commenced, it should be allowed to take its course, so as not to interfere with the gratification. Anyone who has a conscious or unconscious feeling of guilt associated with masturbation will not be able to follow this rule until he or she goes to a sex counseling clinic or confides in someone who has sympathy for such matters. For the feeling of guilt caused by masturbation is only increased by not talking about it and keeping the problem to oneself. The following are examples of harmful masturbatory practices: stimulation without orgasm (in the boy, this means holding back ejaculation); prolonging stimulation by interrupting masturbation too frequently or by failing to provide further stimulation; attempting to bring about an erection in a flaccid penis when no sexual excitation exists; in the case of girls, masturbating in the vagina with a sharp or pointed object (this happens quite frequently); mutual stimulation between boy and girl, girl and girl, or boy and boy without permitting orgasm.

Consciously or unconsciously, sexual fantasies are always linked with masturbation. As long as the boy or the girl masturbates while fantasizing about genital intercourse or about kisses and embraces, there is no cause for alarm. If, however, in the course of masturbation, fantasies involving beating someone or being beaten and similar content begin to crop up, then the youth should initially discuss this with an older friend, unless he can manage unaided to find a partner for sexual intercourse. Undisturbed, satisfying sexual intercourse is usually the best remedy against such incipient sexual problems.

Many young people are afraid that by masturbating they will damage their genitals or later become impotent. We can say, with complete certainty, that as long as masturbation takes place without any disruption and with complete gratification and release of tension, there is no need to fear any danger either now or in the future. The period of time during which masturbation is enjoyed as a satisfactory experience varies from individual to individual. For example, masturbation is problematical right from the start in a person who approaches sex with feelings of guilt and anxiety because of the sexual education he has received from early childhood. Another person may be able to tolerate onanistic gratification for several years without any damage before it ceases to afford him complete release of tension. In a third person, the state of dissatisfaction during and after masturbation sets in very rapidly, and from a purely medical standpoint the only advice we can offer in such a case is this: As soon as masturbation no longer fulfills its function of providing gratification, as soon as it starts to be associated with disgust, guilt feelings, and unpleasure, the young person should not be afraid of moving on to sexual intercourse. However, as young people know from their own experience, most of them are not really in a position to follow this particular piece of medical advice, because the existing sexual rules of our society make intercourse between adolescents difficult. We realize that it is nonsense to set a precise age limit between maturity and immaturity, e.g., to say that up to the age of sixteen a youth may not indulge in sexual intercourse, while from the sixteenth birthday onward this activity is permitted. A boy who can get by with masturbation until he is seventeen or eighteen is doing relatively well. If, however, a boy or a girl who reaches full physical and emotional maturity at an earlier age can no longer tolerate masturbation and is unable to drown out the urge to have intercourse, then we face a major problem, not only in each individual case but also from the standpoint of the masses of these young people. These young people experience even more keenly the more or less hidden disadvantages of masturbation over sexual intercourse. Not only is their feeling of unpleasure and disgust afterward greater, but the dangers associated with unsatisfactory masturbation increase. Let me list some of them: If the young person is unable for external or internal reasons to take the step to sexual intercourse and to a mature sexual life, his development is blocked and it is easy for him to start to slip backwards, i.e., to have recourse to childish fantasies that lead him away from the naturally given goal that now exists. We observe that various drives then increase in intensity. For example, the inclination toward persons of the same sex increases; the social barriers preventing sexual intercourse and the separation of the sexes are the major reasons for excessive indulgence in mutual masturbation among young people of the same sex. The lascivious desire to look at naked bodies or to expose one's own sex organs and the temptation to have sexual relations with children also often occur for the first time at this stage. Because of pent-up sexual energy, which finds no satisfactory release, sadistic and masochistic tendencies, which are usually attenuated and kept in the background by the development of normal sexual activity, now become fully effective. It is certainly not our intention to frighten anybody by pointing out such things. We merely wish to state that the foundation for such disturbances can be laid by preventing young people from having normal sexual relations at a time when they urgently need them. We cannot ignore the facts and must fight with all means available against the sexual rules of society that cause such damage in young people. We must use all our force to make them understand that their struggle with masturbation, their feelings of guilt, their sexual deviations, are not their fault nor are they inherited; instead, they are for the most part the consequences of a society's rules governing sexual behavior which force the development and the natural course of sexuality into one mold into which it is impossible for all young people to fit.

From the standpoint of sexual hygiene, masturbation during puberty, as compared to sexual intercourse, has a number of disadvantages. It forces the young person to direct his sexual desires toward himself, makes it easier for him to obtain gratification, and thus weakens his drive to seek out a sexual partner and to develop his body and mind in the struggle to find such a partner. It is the reason why an enormous number of young people, boys as well as girls, are lonely, because given the social barriers in the way of sexual intercourse, the period during which masturbation is practiced extends in most cases beyond the time when it is harmless. The risk of lapsing into daydreams and of losing interest in the major social questions of the world is linked with masturbation, perhaps not in the initial phase, but certainly the risk increases the longer the practice is continued. In addition, whenever a society does everything it can to keep the sexes apart, it virtually encourages homosexual masturbation among young men and women, creating precisely the situation which it then deplores. There is one final disadvantage that arises when a person indulges in masturbation for too long without making the transition to intercourse, and we should mention it here. Many young people who are weary of masturbation are unable for internal or external reasons (sexual inhibitions, shyness, bashfulness, lack of money, overwhelming poverty) to have sexual intercourse. If they also reject homosexual activity, they end up at the age of seventeen, eighteen, or nineteen, i.e., precisely when their sexuality is beginning to flourish, gradually suppressing that sexuality and their sexual thoughts. As a result, they prepare the way for a sexual dysfunction at some later date, impaired potency or impaired sensations during intercourse, and so often lay the foundation for emotional disturbances.

The vast majority of the sexual problems that we encounter in the sex-counseling centers (about 80 percent of the people seeking advice have such problems) can be traced to disturbances of sexual life during childhood, to suppression of sexual activity during puberty, or to long periods of abstinence following a long or short period of masturbation during puberty.

In summary, we must say that masturbation during puberty is probably the best outlet for adolescents given the current conditions affecting their sexual lives. However, this does not hold true for more than a certain period of time. Also, it does not apply to all young people, because many of them need intercourse much earlier; and others, probably the majority, cannot benefit from masturbation as a way out of their problems, because they are already so damaged by the sexual suppression to which they were subjected during childhood that they are incapable of permitting themselves to masturbate without feelings of guilt.

Masturbation is thus by no means the solution to the problem of adolescent sexuality, as many people believe.

The sex act

Before we deal with the problems which the sexual rules of our society create for young people wanting to have sexual intercourse, we must discover how sexual gratification is obtained during the sex act under natural conditions, as, for example, among the youth of matrilineal-primitive peoples, and also in some healthy young people in our own culture.

The sex act, of which the young person becomes capable on reaching puberty and to which he is normally impelled, if he has not suppressed his sexual excitation and thoughts, is initiated by the erection of the penis in the male and by excitation of the female sex organs. As already mentioned, this preparatory stage is brought about by increased blood flow through the sex organs. Let us try to plot a curve of the phases of the sex act in a healthy human being (Figure 1). Physical and emotional tension is at a certain level. Before the act is commenced, this tension is increased by mutual caresses, kisses, touching, stroking, and other love play for which no moral rules can be set.

If intercourse is commenced immediately without any foreplay, the existing sexual excitation is only partially developed and the partners are dissatisfied afterward; the girl in particular suffers. Therefore, a hasty sexual act performed without undressing, at the first opportunity that presents itself, is usually followed by a feeling of aversion and disgust. In love play it should be remembered—and healthy people do not need to be told this—that kissing the nipples and earlobes and *gently* stroking the labia minora and the clitoris greatly increases excitation in the

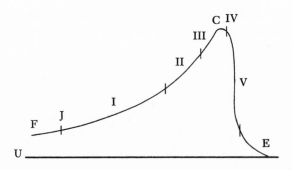

FIGURE 1. *Curve Depicting Excitation during Normal Sexual Intercourse between a Man and a Woman*

U   line representing unexcited state
F   forepleasure—foreplay
J   start of intercourse
I   phase of voluntary control of excitation
II   increase in excitation and transition to involuntary increase in stimulation
III   sudden and steep ascent to climax
C   start of climax
IV   orgasm
V   drop in excitation—release of tension
E   excitation ebbs away until person feels completely relaxed

woman and thus helps her achieve complete gratification. Many women shy away from caressing the male organ; this disturbs the sexual harmony of many couples. There is little point in describing all the various kinds of love play. People who can rid themselves of their sexual inhibitions discover by themselves what their partners desire. Sexual skills cannot be learned from books. All you need to know is that nothing is immoral as long as it causes no harm and helps one's partner to experience greater pleasure.

The sex act itself is begun by slowly introducing the

penis into the vagina. In the first phase (I), both partners
are able to control their excitation and to increase or check
it at will. The vagina becomes slippery so that the intro-
duction and movement of the male organ inside it is not
painful but pleasurable. The slower and the more gentle
this movement, the greater is the pleasure which ultimately
leads to complete sexual satisfaction. In our culture, the
usual position for intercourse is with the woman lying on
her back, legs spread wide apart, and the man on top of
her, supporting his weight on his knees and elbows. Among
some primitive peoples the act is also performed in a
crouching position. There is no reason to be morally out-
raged if another position is adopted, for example, if the
girl sits astride the boy or if the act is performed from the
rear or from the side. People are free to choose their posi-
tions because they cannot hurt anyone, provided that both
partners are in agreement and derive satisfaction. Both
partners move their pelvises back and forth, thereby trans-
ferring more and more of the general tension in their
bodies to their sexual parts, until a certain peak is reached.
From then on the excitation can no longer be controlled
(II and III). If both partners are completely healthy, they
feel that they are being overwhelmed by the excitation and
that they are neither willing nor able to control it any
longer. The climax, which now follows, is heralded in the
boy by the urge to ejaculate and in the girl by the impulse
to take the male organ completely into her body. The
points in the curve where it rises steeply (III) and then
suddenly plunges again even more steeply (IV and V) before gradually subsiding (E) indicate the phase of climax.
Thus, a sexual climax consists of a sudden increase in
excitation to the point where consciousness is partially
obliterated. This is followed by a feeling of satisfaction and

relaxation. It is easy to understand that any interruption or disruption precisely during this final phase of intercourse, e.g., withdrawing the penis as a method of preventing pregnancy (coitus interruptus), or having to watch out that nobody intrudes at this particular moment, etc., must inevitably have negative effects on the general state of health of the sexual partners.

After gratification—and it is most complete when both partners reach a climax together or one partner "comes" shortly after the other—they feel relaxed, calm, tired without being exhausted. Each partner feels very tender toward the other, and if the possibility exists, they lapse into deep, peaceful sleep. When they wake up they feel strengthened, happy, and full of energy, and their self-confidence is reinforced. After releasing sexual tension, a person is no longer distracted by sexual needs and can devote himself freely to his work. Satisfying intercourse is also important for the body as a whole, because the vigorous circulation of blood through all the tissues promotes metabolic activity. This explains the fresh, robust appearance of the person who is sexually satisfied, compared with the usually pale, pasty appearance of the abstinent person.

The natural phases of intercourse which we have discussed will strike some people as very strange. Many will feel that with them it is not all that smooth and trouble-free. We will discuss why this is so, why it does not go smoothly, why these people find everything so strange, and why in fact intercourse is so different nowadays. The undisturbed course of the sexual act as we have described it is not a fantasy but does occur, although rarely in young people in our culture, whereas it is the rule among young people in a primitive society.

Disturbances affecting intercourse

It is apparent from the questions that young people ask that they are interested in little else except sexual dysfunctions, and rightly so, because a great many young people suffer from them. It is necessary to have a clear understanding of the fact that what we are dealing with here is a question of education, i.e., in the final analysis, a question about our innermost life. Some of these disturbances which, if they last too long, can destroy the lives of many young people or at least make them unfit for work, are easy to eliminate *in the early stages* if we fully understand their nature, whereas if we do not understand the circumstances correctly, they can develop into permanent disorders. Therefore, although our space is limited, we must at least discuss their basic characteristics.

There are three essential types of disturbances from which the boy suffers and an equal number that affect the girl. In the case of the male they are:

1. *Inadequate or incomplete erection, i.e., impotence.* Except for the few cases in which this condition is somatically based, the cause is usually due to unconscious fear of intercourse or to shyness toward the female sex organs. Consciously, this fear and shyness are generally manifested in feelings of sexual inferiority. Very often the ideology of abstinence is based on disturbed potency. The person believes that he does not wish to have intercourse for moral reasons, whereas in reality he is merely afraid of intercourse. Impotence can be eliminated by making the sufferer aware of these unconscious anxieties. In the early stages of impotence the problem is often just one of general shyness toward the opposite sex caused by the person's education, which generates anxieties that inhibit the course of sexual excitation. Impotence then comes about because

the boy believes he is faced with a very difficult task when he wants to have sexual intercourse with a girl. This merely increases his fear; but if one is afraid, it is not possible to become sexually excited. Usually, in order to prove to himself and the girl that he is not impotent, the boy nevertheless tries to have intercourse and, of course, under such circumstances he is unsuccessful. Girls, for their part, tend to laugh at the boy in such cases, and this merely increases his shyness and feeling of impotence. He really does become gradually disturbed if he allows himself to be overcome by this feeling. Such incipient inhibitions occur very frequently in otherwise quite healthy adolescents, and they are often easy to remove if the boy does not try to do precisely the wrong thing, namely, to have intercourse even if he does not really want to, or is afraid to. An erection can never be willed, because it is the result of an unconscious emotional process, and any deliberate intention or forcing will merely achieve the opposite effect. If, when he is too worked up and afraid, the boy does nothing except lie still and wait, and if the girl is not stupid enough to laugh at him—for which again our sexual education would be to blame, because it often makes sexuality a matter of ambition—then sooner or later the erection will return if the boy is healthy in all other respects.

Because of the general attitude of society, of physicians, and of the Church toward masturbation, most adolescents believe that this practice is the reason for their impotence. This is incorrect. Undisturbed and satisfying masturbation never leads to impotence. The problem always lies with the feelings of anxiety and guilt that are linked with masturbation because of our morals and education, thus intensifying the sexual shyness and setting the stage for potency problems. The best way to deal with these problems is to wait until erections occur easily in suitable circumstances and anxiety is reduced. Once the boy has experienced pleasure in the sexual act, his potency increases with regular intercourse. It should be stressed once more that nothing could be worse for slight inhibitions in the early stages than despair or trying to force things. If people would just do something about these adolescent problems, there would be no suicides committed for these reasons, there would be no unhappiness, and initial inhibitions would not develop in intensity to the stage where the person becomes completely impotent.

In many cases, deep-rooted emotional disturbances are involved. There are nowhere nearly enough treatment facilities for the enormous number of sexually disturbed people. Also, physicians have received little or no training at our universities in questions of sexuality. Consequently, they usually know nothing about it or do entirely the wrong thing. Blame for impaired potency can be ascribed to the sexually suppressive education which begins when ignorant parents discover their small child masturbating, which it normally does as a matter of course, and then threaten it with all manner of punishment, such as cutting off the penis, tying the hands, invoking the devil and God, who of course see everything. This is the first serious blow against the child's future potency and sexual health.

2. *Premature ejaculation.* What happens in this case is that the boy, instead of being able to control his ejaculation for a certain period of time during intercourse (five to fifteen minutes), "comes," either before the penis enters the vagina or very soon afterward. Premature ejaculation prevents full release of sexual tension, as is obvious from Figure 2. There is no time for the sexual excitation to concentrate in the sex organ; therefore, the existing excitation cannot be fully discharged. Another consequence of premature ejaculation is of course that the girl's need for grati-

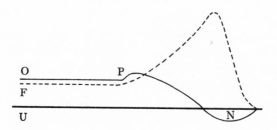

FIGURE 2. *Curve Depicting Premature Ejaculation*

Broken line = normal excitation
U   line representing unexcited state
F   forepleasure
O   overexcitation (usually caused by fear of intercourse)
P   penetration of penis; ejaculation follows soon after;
     excitation cannot increase and gratification is not
     achieved
N   unpleasure following ejaculation

fication is denied. This is another disturbance that is caused
by the suppression of a person's sexual life during childhood and the creation of sexual anxiety. In many cases it is
very easy to eliminate or minimize the problem by correct
behavior. Often the difficulty is caused by attempting intercourse in anxious haste, which may be related to the fear
of being discovered, or by too much stimulation beforehand, or by being fully clothed. Frequently, premature
ejaculation is simply the result of not having intercourse
often enough. Depending on the cause, the problem can be
eliminated by not hurrying the act but instead initiating it
slowly and carefully, by being not fully clothed but naked,
by not overdoing stimulation beforehand, and by having
intercourse as often as necessary. Young people will justifi-
ably say at this point that it is all very well to give such ad-

vice, but what should they do if there is no opportunity for sexual intercourse without clothes and without being disturbed; and what if the conditions in which our youth live force them to be content with satisfying their sexual needs rarely rather than not at all? By replying in this manner young people are merely saying themselves what we have always asserted, namely, that the struggle to achieve a satisfactory sexual life can only be successful in conjunction with the fight against social inequalities and sexual reactionism. We must also establish sex-counseling centers for young people where they are not merely given contraceptive devices but are properly educated in social and sexual matters. This is necessary in order to increase their aggressiveness and their intellectual alertness, which are undermined by material want but even more so by sexual problems.

3. *Disturbance of the ability to experience gratification.* If an adolescent's capacity to have an erection is disturbed or if he suffers from premature ejaculation, naturally his gratification is impaired. However, frequently the young man is basically healthy and merely fails to experience proper release of tension in the phase of end-pleasure. This inability is linked primarily to inhibitions resulting from modern methods of upbringing that prevent the young person from abandoning himself completely. It also has something to do with the circumstances under which youths have sexual intercourse. It is utterly impossible to experience appropriate release of tension and gratification when the sex act is attempted fully clothed or in the presence of third parties, or in constant fear of being interrupted. In addition, partly because of inner emotional problems, but also because of their miserable social position, young people are often unable to develop a relationship to the point that mutual sexual adjustment comes about. Adoles-

cents frequently change partners once they become sexually active, and we should judge this fact not morally but medically. Constant changing of partners makes sexual adaptation impossible and thus excludes the possibility of experiencing complete gratification of sensual and tender desires in the sexual act. This is not to be interpreted as meaning that we support the old notion of everlasting faithfulness and frown on changing partners. In fact, we believe that such a position is quite untenable. However, we must distinguish between partner changing and partner changing, for there are various criteria by which we must judge and comment on this activity.

Often a boy or a girl has to look around for some time before finding a suitable partner, sleeping with this or that person and then looking some more. There is no reason to condemn this, because the belief that one can recognize the right person at first sight is not all that far removed from the ecclesiastical view that one should first bind oneself forever to one's partner at the altar of God before having carnal knowledge of the other, even though ninety-nine times out of one hundred one is "buying a pig in a poke."

It is necessary to change partners whenever sexual compatibility does not exist or breaks down, or if a serious relationship with someone else develops. Such a change is usually a more or less painful process for the other partner involved. But the healthier the former partner is, the sooner he or she will be able to overcome the separation. The more dependent one partner is on the other due to upbringing or circumstances, and this is particularly the case nowadays where girls are concerned, the more he or she will suffer. It is therefore a good idea not to enter into any sexual relationship if it is obvious that a future separation would be a catastrophic event for the other person.

During adolescence, the pace and manner of psychic

development vary so greatly that, with time, problems will occur in a relationship that force the partners to separate. There are also morbid reasons for changing partners: the inability to stay with a partner for a long period of time; the total inability to experience sexual gratification; suppressed and repressed homosexuality, which disrupts any relationship with a partner of the opposite sex or prevents the relationship from deepening. Partners are sometimes also quickly changed out of ambition ("I must have 'had' so and so many boys/girls"). Such an attitude is not only damaging to the person who holds it but also to all other people involved. If, for example, a boy sleeps with one girl after another, the girls suffer badly. A boy who behaves like this is usually sexually disturbed. It is just as unhealthy, damaging, and a sign of our moribund sexual conditions when a girl, out of ambition or a desire for power, deliberately attracts many boys to herself and then plays with them like a cat with a mouse, not treating any of them seriously and merely taking pleasure in teasing them without becoming a sexual friend of any of them. In such cases there is always something wrong with the girl; love is replaced by the desire to dominate.

If we say that a person is often forced to sleep with this or that person in order to find a suitable partner, this statement should not be raised to the level of a theory. It is a fact that a healthy boy or girl whose sexuality has fully developed can usually tell beforehand whether a girl or a boy is suited for them. Of course, wrong choices can still be made. There are so many factors on which sexual adaptation and gratification depend that it is impossible to determine them all precisely, e.g., ability to develop attitudes of mutual friendship, temperament, common interests, rhythm of sexual needs, etc. Besides, our sex education has made these factors so enormously complicated by crippling sexuality from childhood on that problems are the rule and a calm, well-ordered, satisfying sex life is the exception.

If we wish to bring the sexual interests of youths into harmony with their great future-shaping tasks, to which we assign primary importance, then young people must gain access to a well-ordered and satisfactory sex life. However, as a rule this cannot be achieved by swearing eternal faithfulness or by sleeping with all and sundry. Again, we do not wish to establish any moral principles here because they would never succeed, and counter to the view held by many people, we maintain that it is not necessary to feel uncomfortable or even to condemn young people if they occasionally "kick over the traces." Nor will we condemn or despise anyone who is capable of living according to the principle of eternal faithfulness. Let me say it once more: Our sole duty is to gather all our strength and courage for the battle to fully develop the creative urges and the will to live displayed by young people, and we must wage this battle all the way through to final victory. As far as the questions of sexual life are concerned, all we have to do is to offer each other mutual assistance in solving young people's difficulties.

Girls as well as boys, and for the same reasons, exhibit a number of disturbances, although they are much more serious than in the case of boys, as we will attempt to show with the aid of the curve in Figure 3. Here we see the broken line which indicates the undisturbed, fully satisfying course of sexual excitation in the girl, and four other curves, which represent various dysfunctions.

1. *Complete lack of sexual feeling, i.e., frigidity.* This is usually associated with pain or considerable unpleasure for the girl in the sexual act. This condition is depicted by curve A. Such girls not only fail to experience gratification

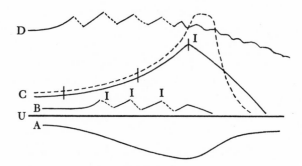

FIGURE 3. *Curves Depicting Genital Disturbances in Women*

Broken line = normal sensations
U line representing unexcited state
A complete lack of sensation in the vagina and unpleasure (pain, disgust) during intercourse; instead
of pleasure, the sexual act is a source of unpleasure
B inadequate sensitivity; because of inhibitions (I) the
excitation cannot increase; gratification is never experienced
C normal sensitivity at the start of intercourse; the inhibitions (I) commence just before the climax is
reached; end-pleasure is only inadequately experienced, if at all
D disturbed sexuality in the case of nymphomania; from
the start, the excitation is much higher than normal
but cannot rise or fall; gratification is not experienced;
the state of sexual excitation is often stronger afterward than before

during intercourse but, what is more, they avoid it and feel
sick at the thought of it. Their genital sexuality is completely suppressed by unconscious fear or rejection of the
male, and it is often overlain by homosexual and masculine
tendencies. Very often, however, it is merely a superficial
disturbance which sooner or later disappears if the boy is
potent and knows how to arouse the girl's sexuality during

intercourse. Such girls include many who are totally lacking in vaginal sensation but have an oversensitive clitoris. Outwardly, they often behave in a very sexual manner, but in reality they are afraid of intercourse and avoid it.

2. Curve B depicts the condition of *inadequate vaginal sensation*. Although the girl experiences a certain amount of pleasure during intercourse, she cannot experience gratification.

3. Curve C depicts the special case in which a girl at first experiences quite normal sensations during intercourse but they die away *before* release. This is often due to fear of the excitation that suddenly increases just before climax and clouds the consciousness to some extent. In many girls this manifests itself in the belief that something terrible might happen to them in the process. Thus, such girls experience pleasure up to a certain point but never attain the proper, normal release of tension. Both types of disturbance, B and C, require treatment, or they may recede in time if the boy proceeds skillfully and gently enough and shows a great deal of consideration. It is necessary to issue a serious warning against trying to treat such disturbances as vaginismus, which denotes a reflex-like defensive reaction of the girl against the penetration of the male organ, by some mechanical means. She always entertains great fears about intercourse. Thus such a procedure as dilation of the vaginal opening, which is sometimes attempted, far from being helpful, intensifies the girl's sexual anxiety because it is associated with pain.

4. Curve D depicts the following disturbance: The girl is overexcited and seems to experience a great deal of sexual satisfaction in intercourse. But this is not the case. She merely experiences a certain level of excitation which cannot rise to the point of release, or drop with gratification. Such girls are always very unhappy and suffer intensely

because they exist in a state of constant undischarged sexual excitation. They are usually "man-crazy," as it is so aptly put, and play a disruptive role in the sexual lives of young men, because they pursue any young man who is reasonably attractive. These girls should not be condemned or despised, because they are usually the victims of a complex and tortuous sexual education, and they require intensive psychiatric care. If their sexual disturbance is eliminated, they become capable once more of experiencing gratification and their nymphomania immediately disappears. This may happen as a result of a course of treatment or because of some special sexual experience or through the birth of a child. However, whoever condemns such women is himself biased and moralistic. If they disturb a group or organization, they must be talked to in a friendly manner and they must be helped.

Sexual disturbances are in general much more widespread in girls and women than in boys and men. This is fully in keeping with the fact that from childhood onward women are far more sexually suppressed in our society, and they also receive a much stricter sexual education than boys.

Venereal diseases and how to prevent them

Venereal diseases are infectious. The only difference between them and other infectious diseases is that they are not so easily transmitted. While influenza or tuberculosis, for example, can be transmitted simply by coughing, transmission of a venereal disease requires intimate contact such as occurs during intercourse. The most dangerous kind of venereal disease, syphilis, can also be transmitted by kissing.

The most frequent of the venereal diseases is gonorrhea. Three to fourteen days after being infected, the man is aware of an itching in the urethra and a burning sensation

on urination, and a purulent discharge appears. In the
woman the discharge is heavy, and she has problems urinating. However, the symptoms may be negligible or completely lacking. Although gonorrhea is often harmless and
can be cured within three to six weeks,* if it is not treated
promptly, complications are likely: the bladder and the
adjacent glands may become affected, as well as the epi-
didymis and the fallopian tubes. Inflammation of the epi-
didymis and of the fallopian tubes frequently leads to their
occlusion and, if it occurs bilaterally, which is often the
case, results in childlessness. Gonorrheal inflammation of
the pelvic organs is also the cause of many female complaints.

The second disease, which usually has a harmless course,
is the soft chancre (chancroid), which appears two to
three days after infection. Usually several superficial purulent ulcers form, which disappear within a few days if they
are correctly treated.† One unpleasant complication of this
disease is sometimes a painful inflammation of the inguinal
glands, known as bubo, which may fester and have to be
aspirated.

The soft chancre may appear coincident with a hard
chancre and initially conceal it. Otherwise, the hard chancre appears two to three weeks after infection and represents the start of syphilis. It manifests itself as a weeping
sore which gradually becomes hard and raised. If treatment is commenced immediately upon discovery or within
the first six weeks after infection, the pathogen is destroyed. The chancre itself will heal without treatment,
but in that case a skin eruption will appear and the blood

* Today, of course, with use of antibiotics, the therapeutic response is
far more rapid and effective, although a new problem has arisen due to
infection by a more resistant strain of organism.—*Eds.*

† Sulfonamides are the appropriate drugs used today.—*Eds.*

as well as the entire body will be invaded by the spirochete, leading even after several years to growths or serious lesions of the nervous system (brain and spinal cord). The latter were formerly treated with malaria, but now with penicillin (or other antibiotics if the person is penicillin-sensitive).*

As far as avoiding venereal diseases is concerned, the most important point to remember is that you should never enter into sexual relationships with people whom you know little about. If there is indication of sexual contact with an infected person, treatment should be sought immediately. It is particularly important to go to the doctor if one notices a discharge or sore on the genitals. Only a specialist or a counseling center run by a specialist can judge whether it is a harmless inflammation, an incipient case of gonorrhea, an abrasion, or a chancre. Incipient gonorrhea as well as hard chancre can be nipped in the bud if treatment is commenced in good time; but you should not wait, particularly in the case of gonorrhea.

Venereal diseases are almost never transmitted out of maliciousness but only as a result of carelessness and ignorance. At the moment of intercourse the infecting partner usually does not know that he or she is infectious. It is possible to transmit the disease in the period between becoming infected and the outbreak of symptoms. Therefore, you should never have sexual intercourse with somebody whose name and address you do not know.

It is extremely important to educate young people about the nature and prevention of venereal disease, but proper education in such matters will not come about until the world has changed in the way that we want it to. Educating

---

* The incidence of later stages of syphilis has been declining, even without the indicated specific treatment, because antibiotics are now so frequently used for other infectious diseases as well.—*Eds.*

people about venereal diseases in the manner it is done now is a public danger because it fills people's minds with enormous fear of sexuality in general, forces them to be abstinent, and creates innumerable cases of hypochondria and anxiety states.

Self-regulation of sexual life through gratification

People everywhere nowadays are racking their brains to find ways to eliminate the sexual morass, the sexual misery, the murders and suicides, the grief and the unhappiness that arise in vast quantities from sexual problems. New moral precepts are constantly being prescribed; responsibility is preached; many young people are being condemned and sent to jail for committing sexual crimes; and yet the simplest fact itself is not understood, namely, that as long as people's sexual lives are suppressed there will of necessity be sexual crime, anguish, and misery. We will examine later the reason for this sexual suppression, which causes so much distress, but we can already state the obvious: just as a starving person is capable of theft, so anyone whose needs are satisfied does not steal. Among primitive peoples there is no word for theft; the concept is simply unknown. Theft and murder committed in the course of theft do not appear in the history of human society until the emergence of hunger and suppression, and the same is true of sexual crimes. Among those primitive peoples who lead satisfactory, unimpaired sexual lives, there is no sexual crime, no sexual perversion, no sexual brutality between man and woman; rape is unthinkable because it is unnecessary in their society. Their sexual activity flows in normal, well-ordered channels which would fill any cleric with indignation and fear, because the pale, ascetic youth and the gossiping, child-beating woman do not exist in these primitive societies. They love the human body and take pleasure in their sexuality. They do not understand why young men and women should not enjoy their sexuality. But when their lives are invaded by the ascetic, hypocritical morass and by the Church, which bring them "culture" along with exploitation, alcohol, and syphilis, they begin to suffer the same wretchedness as ourselves. They begin to lead "moral" lives, i.e., to suppress their sexuality, and from then on they decline more and more into a state of sexual distress, which is the result of sexual suppression. At the same time, they become sexually dangerous; murders of spouses, sexual diseases, and crimes all start to appear. Whereas earlier they committed no sexual crimes because it was not necessary, they start now to commit such acts because they are driven to do so by the sexual craving that is generated in them.

It is a fact that *only the person who is incapable of gratification, the person whose sexual life is impeded and disturbed and who is contaminated by moral inhibitions, becomes sexually dangerous, while the sexually gratified and healthy person, no matter how many and what relationships he has, poses no risk to social coexistence.* We can judge this from our own experience. Who among us knows a healthy, sexually satisfied adult who seduces or even murders children in order to gratify his lust on their corpses? Who among us knows any sexually healthy men or boys who rape women or, except in periods of special sexual distress, resort to prostitutes? Who among us knows of a girl or woman whose sexuality is fully developed, and who knows what sexual gratification means in terms of health and vigor, who throws herself willy-nilly at the first acceptable man who comes along? None of us do, because it just does not happen. Sexual gratification, the regular release of sexual tension, together with work that is not excessively exhausting, will automatically regulate a person's sex life in a healthy manner. Can the basic conditions of a natural, pleasurable sex life be fulfilled? They can:

1. If we organize and structure our work on the basis of the natural pleasure that we have in that work.

2. If we create the necessary preconditions for a natural and healthy life, destroy the hypocrisy among us, create adequate housing, reach an understanding with the older members of society about what young people need in life and remind them of their own youth; also, if we create a natural relationship between work and happy, sensibly spent leisure hours; in brief, if we actually put into practice the things about which we talk and think so much.

3. If we free ourselves from our inner bonds. That means no longer experiencing the sex act as a valueless event on the same level as the evacuation of the bowels and replacing the craving and lust in ourselves with a natural desire for love. Then the crimes, violent abductions, and sexual murders of children would cease.

Abstinence and work productivity

One of the most important objections which sexologists and researchers into the problems of youth raise against sexual intercourse among young people, and which make them demand that young people should practice abstinence, is the notion that sexual intercourse would, to use their terms, impair young people's "cultural" and other achievements. The attitude of these opponents of sexual intimacy between young people can be summarized approximately as follows: You have 100 percent sexual energy. Sexual energy can be diverted and used for various nonsexual purposes. If you divert 10 percent of it to your work, that isn't enough. If you divert 30 percent, that is getting better; 60 percent is better still; but best of all, you should use the full 100 percent in your work, because then you would not only achieve the maximum work output because you do not "live out" your impulses but you would also avoid many of the problems that young people face when they engage in a sexual life today. This "100 percent position," which is in favor of diverting all sexual energy and putting it to some other use, is, first, factually incorrect and, second, moralistic, because the people who hold this opinion are merely evading the objectively correct response to the problem. The fact is that young people's greatest problems come about precisely because sexual intercourse is stifled by education and by the entire set of sexual rules in our society; also, nothing is achieved by preaching behavioral attitudes that cannot be put into practice. Let us not fool ourselves! This particular viewpoint has never been fully accepted, nor will it ever be. There is no reason why anyone should accept it. The argument is essentially false because, even if it is true that sexual interests can be temporarily neglected (entirely for a short time, only partly for longer periods of time), total sublimation over extended periods of time is harmful. *If the sublimation goes too far, the encouragement of non-sexual, social, and scientific interests and the stimulation of the work capacity of young people will backfire, and the suppressed sexual drives will begin to disturb the work.* Let us, therefore, put forward a view which we can prove is more correct. Up to a certain point, sexual energy and sexual tension can be converted into work, or into social and scientific interest, but beyond that point the inhibition of sexual gratification disrupts the ability to work. There are various reasons for this:

After a period of abstinence during which a person has

succeeded in immersing himself in some kind of important work which drowns out the sexual urges and absorbs his sexual energy, the process of sublimation begins to lose ground in the average youth, and sexual fantasies, consciously or unconsciously, increasingly force their way to the surface. Experience shows that the ability to work becomes more and more disturbed the more unconscious sexual fantasies are, because greater amounts of psychic energy are needed to keep them in check. This decrease in the ability to work manifests itself as an inability to pay attention to what one is doing (daydreaming), lack of concentration, "poor memory," as young people call it, feelings of listlessness, nervousness, restlessness. *The remaining sexual interests which cannot be sublimated, but instead drive the person to seek gratification, disrupt the work.* The more the young person attempts to immerse himself in his work to compensate for the disruption, the more he tries to pull himself together, and the more he reproaches himself, the more difficult it is for him to do so. His daydreaming and fantasies trouble him immensely, but he is unable to control them, and even if he makes a supreme effort, he is only successful in suppressing them for a short time. Practical experience gathered in sex-counseling centers shows conclusively that if such a youth renounces abstinence soon enough, either by starting to masturbate or by commencing sexual intercourse, the work disturbances disappear immediately. We shall see later that this remedy is very difficult, if not impossible, for most young people living under the conditions of our society.

It is true that a few actually do manage to shake off the problems of sexual life for many years by devoting themselves to work of some kind or another. And the advocates of abstinence always point to these successful few. But in the interest of good health, we must condemn such a standpoint here, because we have to deal with the mass of young people as a whole and not with just a few of them, and the majority are *not* successful in practicing abstinence over protracted periods of time.

Many people point to sports as a means of diverting sexual interests. It is certainly correct that sports help young people to cope with the problem to some extent and for a period of time, because the increased muscular activity consumes sexual energy. But if, like the medical counselors of young people in sex-counseling centers, you have seen the many strong athletes who, at the age of twenty-five, twenty-eight, thirty, come and complain that they have some sexual disturbance or some other symptom of a nervous disorder, you will understand immediately that anyone who, seemingly without difficulty, practices abstinence in his youthful years is in fact putting himself at extremely great risk later in life. Therefore, the preaching of abstinence must be vigorously opposed purely from the medical standpoint. The moralists, however, only have eyes for what occasionally, in their opinion, confirms their theory. They do not see and do not even want to see that their doctrines do not apply to the mass of young people, and they duck responsibility for what will happen in the future if people follow their teachings. What will then happen to the sexual apparatus is what happens to any organ that is prevented for long periods of time from performing its natural activity: it atrophies.

We therefore hold the view that, in principle, the sexual needs of young people cannot be solved without affirmation and concern for their sex lives, without gratifying sexual intercourse. We should not forget that the hypocrisy and philistinism that have developed over the millennia are also deeply rooted in ourselves. We must, therefore, deal with ourselves as well as with the problems outside ourselves.

ON THE QUESTION OF HOMOSEXUALITY

One often hears it asked whether homosexuality is natural or not, why it is punished, and whether it is really harmful if a person has homosexual relations. In reply to these questions we should ideally set forth the entire debate raging among sexologists and lawyers on the topic. But that would be beyond our scope, and we must therefore limit ourselves to a few main points, particularly to analyzing what our position on this matter is or properly should be.

As most recent scientific research has shown, all human beings are bisexual from the start, not only physically, but, as a function of the physical, emotionally as well. Up until the third month of pregnancy any fetus can develop into a male or a female, because the female and male sex organs with all associated paraphernalia develop simultaneously. In the third month, however, either the male or the female characteristics generally begin to develop, while the characteristics of the other sex fall behind in the developmental process. Those rudimentary characteristics which fail to develop fully never disappear entirely, even though they are not capable of performing any function. For example, the female clitoris is nothing more than a rudimentary male penis and the nipples of a man are undeveloped female breasts.

Now, there are people in whom these usually rudimentary features develop quite a bit further, together with the characteristics of the person's actual sex, so that both sets of sex organs exist side by side or are in some way combined with each other. Such individuals are called "hermaphrodites." There are men with female pelvic structures and female breasts, and there are women who have a fully developed penis. There are also people whose glands contain tissues of the other sex. Usually such hermaphrodites have more or less the same emotions as the opposite sex and they feel sexually attracted to their own sex. However, some of them also have quite different feelings. This puzzle is still very complex and has not been solved.

The people described above, whose homosexuality is physically determined, are in the minority, whereas the majority of all other homosexuals are quite normal as regards their physical form and makeup, i.e., at least according to research conducted so far, the majority of homosexually oriented persons have not developed any physical features of the other sex. When such characteristics are present in the form of manner of expression, gait, and language, an accurate analysis of the persons' emotional development shows that they did not always behave like this but developed these attitudes as a result of the special fate of their sexual drive, and now externally resemble the sex that they do not sexually desire. What is more, there are many men who have the physical and emotional characteristics appropriate to the sex organs with which they are equipped, yet they desire younger, effeminate men toward whom they behave like a man to a wife; and there are completely feminine women who behave toward harder, more masculine-looking women like a wife to a husband. These kinds of homosexuals did not become inclined that way because of physical developments but as a result of defective emotional development in early childhood, when they suffered severe disappointment at the hands of a member of the opposite sex. For example, a male child can easily become openly homosexual if the love he has for his mother is too often and too bitterly disappointed because she is a strict, harsh person. Similarly, a girl can easily be induced to become homosexual at a very early age if she is severely disappointed by her father. Such children readily withdraw their sexual desires from the opposite sex and turn instead to those of their own sex. As a rule, these early disappointments are repressed. Upon growing up, the person who has suffered such disappointments is no longer aware of them and can only recall them when he or she relives this early period of development while undergoing psychiatric treatment.

Both types of homosexuality are thus deviant developments which we must label as illnesses when their homosexuality causes the persons in question to suffer, which is usually the case. It is wrong to believe that this suffering is purely social in nature and is caused by society's persecution of homosexuals. Many homosexuals (it is not possible to say what percentage) are also emotionally and sexually maladjusted in other respects, i.e., they are neurotic. Homosexuals who have settled into this way of life and feel comfortable with it protest against having homosexuality branded as an illness or as the outcome of deviant sexual development. They regard such labeling as a downgrading of their sexual inclinations, and many of them look on themselves as a kind of "third sex," a special sexual category. This view must be denied for purely scientific reasons. Above all, it is necessary to protect young people from turning to homosexuality, not for moral, but for purely sex-economic reasons, because it can be established that even average sexual gratification in heterosexuals is still much more intense than the gratification achieved by homosexuals. And this is very significant in bringing order to a person's psychic economy. The most powerful rebuttal that we can make against the claim made by so many homosexuals that they represent a special kind of sexuality and are not an aberration, is to point out that in the course of a special kind of psychiatric treatment any homosexual can stop feeling the way he or she does, whereas a normally developed person never becomes a homosexual through this same treatment. If the homosexual behavior has not gone on too long and has not totally destroyed relations with the opposite sex, if also the person in question is not happy with the homosexual state and wishes to be rid of it, then homosexuality can be cured fundamentally by treatment, which reverses the aberrant sexual development that occurred in childhood.

What we have said so far is scientifically based fact, and it can be further reinforced by pointing to the example of primitive peoples who lead a satisfying, undisturbed sexual life, who do not hinder the sexual development of their children, and among whom homosexuality is consequently unknown, except in the spiritualized form of friendship. According to the findings of Malinowski, an English ethnologist, homosexuality starts to appear among primitive peoples at the same rate that missionaries import Christian morality into these people's natural sexual lives and separate the sexes from each other. This is also confirmed by the fact, which we observe over and over again, that wherever normal sexual relations between men and women or girls and boys are prohibited or hampered (e.g., in boarding schools, in the army or navy, etc.), homosexuality develops in proportion to the degree of sexual suppression. Thus, ignoring the cases which are physically based, we may provisionally conclude that homosexuality is a purely social phenomenon, i.e., a question of sexual education and development. The best means of preventing it is to bring up and educate the two sexes side by side and to permit sexual intercourse to commence at the right time.

It would be totally wrong, however, to conclude from these facts that homosexuals should be despised or made the object of anti-homosexual campaigns. As long as our system of sexual education permits people to become homosexuals, it is of no concern to anybody if these people lead their lives the way they want, without harming anybody else, and feel comfortable as homosexuals. Confirmation of the fact that homosexuality is a deviant development, and thus not a natural phenomenon, does not give anybody the right to condemn or punish these people. We should try to cure homosexuals who wish to rid themselves of these leanings, either because they are suffering from their condition or because they are not experiencing appropriate gratification, but we should never force them to undergo treatment. Not only do we not have the right to do this, but also any enforced treatment will not succeed. In a class society homosexuality can easily become a serious menace because blackmailers threaten homosexuals with denunciation and thus extort money from them. Blackmail is particularly encouraged by financial distress. There are also many youths who have little money and who consequently sell themselves to homosexuals from the rich strata of society. We should also not underestimate the role that homosexuality plays in political reactionary circles, such as among nationalistic students and officers. Here homosexuality is closely associated with the extremely pronounced moral inhibitions that affect the natural sex lives of these categories of persons.

THE PROBLEMS OF FRIENDSHIP
BETWEEN YOUNG PEOPLE

So far, we have discussed the physical processes that take place during the sex act, and we must now discuss friendship as it exists between girls and boys. The term "friendship," as we shall see in a moment, has quite different

meanings depending on whether it is used by moralists or
by sensible young people.

What does the moralist understand by friendship? If he
really represents the hypocritical sexual order, he cannot
accept that there is such a thing as friendship between the
two sexes. Let us take the example of two average young
people, a boy attending secondary school or high school
and a girl who attends a girls' high school. Because the
double moral standard makes it difficult for him to have
sexual intercourse with girls from his own social group,
the boy's sexuality is split into tenderness and sensuality.
Consequently, there are two kinds of girls for him: one
for physical pleasure and the other for a spiritual relationship. He "venerates" a girl from his own group, and
he hesitates to inflict the humiliation of sexual intercourse
on her, whereas he obtains physical satisfaction from prostitutes. If he loves a girl, he cannot have sexual intercourse
with her, and if he has intercourse with a girl, he cannot
love her. He would also immediately stop loving his "dear-
est" if she had the idea of giving herself to him out of love.
This split in sexuality often goes so far that many youths
are impotent when they have intercourse with a "decent"
girl. If the woman satisfies the man's physical or sensual
side of sexuality *before* marriage, she is an object of sexual
exploitation, particularly since this gratification is often
purchased. *Within* the bonds of marriage, woman becomes
truly the sexual tool of man. Once the "venerated" girl has
married, she soon loses the respect that she once enjoyed,
because, even apart from marital conflicts, the typical man
cannot rid himself of the idea that the sex act is something
that degrades the woman. And sexuality therefore remains
divided in marriage as well; many men continue to satisfy
their sexual needs with other women.

The girl, on the other hand, must suppress her genital sensuality, and instead of natural sexuality, she develops the typical character of the naïve and sentimental woman; she becomes coquettish, sexually overcharged, and obedient, even enslaved, to the man she loves; or she uses her sexuality to dominate men. The elimination of genital gratification results in lasciviousness; such a person must start to exude sexuality from every pore. If a girl of this kind manages to free herself from hypocritical morality and from the hypocritical style of life to lead a sexual life, she concentrates mainly on being sexually stimulating. We then get the phenomenon of the demi-vierge, who does everything, absolutely everything, with the exception of allowing the male organ to enter her vagina.

In none of these cases can we say that friendship exists between boy and girl; nor does it exist between the student and his beloved, nor between man and wife. The man always remains the exploiter of female sexuality; the woman always "gives" and the man always "takes." Sexual life, therefore, always oscillates back and forth between these two contradictions: deification of woman and of love on the one hand, and degradation and besmirching of womanhood and of love on the other.

The splitting of sexuality into debased sensuality and transfigured love, which generates entire systems of philosophy on the problem of "sexuality" and "eroticism," is nothing more than an expression of the dominant position of the man and, in addition, a consequence of the efforts of distinguished hypocrites to set themselves apart from the masses by adopting a special morality. Their own women may be approached sexually only within marriage, and they are accessible only to men from their own social stratum. Sexual intercourse is outlawed outside marriage and with men from lower social strata. The dominance of men has eliminated these restrictions as far as the male sex is concerned. Thus, the sexual act has really become a degradation of the woman, something violent, and women emotionally resist the shame which this act entails for them.

Even the middle class gradually started to become horrified at the consequences of its moral principles. It has never been willing, and never will be, to surrender its principles, but it wants to paper over the filth that it creates. This is done by the liberals and by the liberal women's movement, which originated the idea of "friendship" between man and woman. The woman should no longer be a slave but a "friend of man," not a sexual object but a "companion in life." This was the basis on which the rotten institution of marriage was to be reconstructed. The contrast between "mind" and "body," "tender" and "sensual," "erotic" and "sexual," and the actual degradation of sensuality, led to the rejection of "merely sensual" relationships. Through the moral elimination of tender relationships between man and woman, and through the economic destruction of friendly relationships between man and woman, sensual sexuality was made into something similar to the act of defecation, although this runs counter to all human emotion.

Many people still live with this splintered sexuality, which is downgraded for the man to the level of simple evacuation. A few people, especially groups of intellectuals, have freed themselves from the fetters of hypocritical morality over the years. These are individual cases which are of no interest to us. Despite the fact that they have occasionally achieved friendly sexual relationships, they have no influence on the sexual lives of the masses. As long as education at school and in the home remains the way it is, there can be no true friendship between the sexes.

What do we understand by friendship? Obviously, we reject the notion of dirty sexuality, which is devoid of any tender and friendly relationship and which serves only to release sexual tension, regardless of with whom or where the sexual act is performed. We reject this view not only because it degrades the woman and constitutes an unhealthy form of sexuality, since among other things it is the sexuality of weaklings, but also because we wish to attain complete, healthy sensuality once more. When we comment on physical sexuality we should not forget that nowadays we are no longer dealing with natural physical sexual acts but instead with artificial forms of sexual activity created, distorted, and debased by education. Due to the fact that tenderness is lacking or has been split off, these forms of sexual activity are characterized by lust and lasciviousness beforehand and revulsion, disgust, and abhorrence afterward. *This kind of sexual life is worthless from the standpoint of gratification.* It is therefore wrong to regard this type of "sensual sexuality" as naturally given. Healthy sensuality always goes together with tender and friendly feelings. Anyone who has been able to allow his sexuality to develop unspoiled is incapable of embracing someone genitally unless a personal, tender, or friendly relationship exists between them. It is not true that natural sexuality, that homogeneous, sensual, and tender love, leads to or indeed can ever lead to chaos. Whether sensual attraction leads to friendship or friendship to physical gratification is a matter of indifference to us.

We are convinced that woman is not by nature inferior to man but that over the millennia suppression in the sexual and economic sphere has actually reduced woman to an inferior state. We want not only to eliminate the social and sexual enslavement of women but also to establish the complete emotional friendship of the sexes. Friendship can be understood as either a relationship based on common intellectual interests or a good relationship without such com-

mon interests founded solely on sexual harmony. A boy and
a girl can be good friends without any sexual relationship
existing between them. But it would be wrong to prohibit a
sexual relationship unless friendship based on shared intellectual interests exists. During youth it is very often the
sexual friendship that comes first and leads to emotional
harmony.

The situation is very difficult in another respect as well.
Because of the sexual education which they receive, girls
are much more dependent on boys than the other way
around. For the average girl, a love relationship means not
just a physical but also an emotional relationship, much
more so than it does for the boy. The boy, therefore, incurs
a certain amount of responsibility when he enters into a
relationship with a girl. Because of the material and emotional dependence of the girl, because of the risk of pregnancy and suicide arising from an unhappy love affair, and
for other important reasons, it is essential under the present
conditions of sexual life that this little bit of responsibility,
which has nothing to do with the sentimental preaching of
moralists and babblers about culture, should be retained. As
long as girls and boys are as unclear about sexual matters
and as sexually damaged as we see them today, we must
make it a rule that no boy will force a girl to have intercourse with him; or that if he does enter into a relationship
with a girl, he must know exactly and must have discussed
in detail with her whether she is capable of accepting a
separation without plunging into depression. Naturally, we
reject the notion that a boy must marry a girl once he has
been intimate with her, but on the other hand, we believe
that he should never make anybody miserable. As a rule, a
sexual relationship that has been brought about by force
or by dishonest trickery will not yield the sexual gratification that both sides yearn for. Therefore, the question

should not be judged from a moral, abstract position but from one of sexual strength and health.

Our most important task is to develop to the utmost degree and to maintain in young people a spirit of determination and willingness to fight. Within this context, it is necessary to combat callousness and brutality, because they harm our endeavors by driving a wedge between boy and girl, often turning them into mutual enemies. As young people gradually adopt natural and straightforward views on sexual life, moral warnings of this kind will become superfluous.

Let us reiterate: The easier and more possible it is for people to lead satisfactory and well-ordered love lives, the more such factors as sexual lust and brutality will disappear and the less it will be necessary to remind people constantly to exercise responsibility. Sexual responsibility is automatically present in a healthy, satisfying sexual life. We must still discuss what needs to be done to create the opportunities to lead such a life. Let us not forget that suppression, moralizing, and secretiveness merely create problems without actually impeding sexual intercourse.

There are an infinite number of problems that affect friendships between young people. They are due in part to the disastrous effects exerted by the external conditions of their lives, and in part to their inner sexual helplessness. The *inner* problems, which in the final analysis are created by modern sex education, affect all young people regardless of social strata.

Any person who works with young people knows what represents the greatest problems in sexual relationships between boys and girls: The boys complain that there is never any opportunity to be together without being disturbed, and the girls are unable or unwilling to assume the responsibility of using contraceptives. The boys also complain that the girls make "too much fuss" and have to be wooed for too long, whereas the boys have neither the patience nor the inclination to do this and merely suffer as a result. Many of the girls state that they would be willing to initiate sexual activity themselves, but they are afraid to because the boys usually behave like wild animals and simply pounce on them without showing any concern for them afterward, or they talk badly about the girls among themselves.

These few examples demonstrate clearly the situation as it exists among young people. Neither the boys nor the girls are to blame for this. Instead, it is simply and clearly the result of the contradiction between youthful sexual drives and a sexually suppressive, secretive education. If there was no conflicting morality, and if boys and girls were not sexually suppressed to a great extent, young people would have discovered the truth in good time, namely, that sexual gratification is not simply the gratification of a bodily need like eating or going to the toilet, but that their emotional development, their vitality, their ability to work, and their eagerness to fight for a better life are all determined by the kind of sex life they lead, just as much as by the quality of their material lives. They would have learned that the sexuality of a human being and its gratification at this age is not a joke. Sexual problems would then no longer occur.

Where do these problems originate? The principle of separating the sexes from each other has meant that boys get on better with other boys than with girls. Such boys openly or secretly despise girls, although they feel attracted to them. Girls, on the other hand, feel slighted; they have developed far more sexual anxiety and shyness than boys, although this does not reduce their sexual desires but merely intensifies their conflict with these desires. If boys openly or secretly look down on girls, if many girls are afraid of sexual intercourse, if boys afterward boast among themselves about their experiences and talk badly about girls, and if finally to all this is added the strong sensual attraction of the two sexes and the desire to achieve sexual gratification, then given such contradictory states it is not surprising that boys pounce on girls like wild animals and that girls "make a fuss."

It would be a great mistake to believe that the foregoing are uninteresting private matters, because they are rooted in our sexual order and education; they are destroying young people. These problems, therefore, concern us very much. We must create a freer atmosphere; boys and girls must be able to discuss openly what they think about each other, what they do not like about each other. This will provide the best foundation for genuine as opposed to merely professed friendship between boys and girls.

There are many boys and girls who do not have any morbid inhibitions and who lead well-ordered sex lives, but most young people suffer from disturbed relationships caused by such inhibitions. Sometimes two young people who like each other suffer such strong emotional inhibitions that they do not dare to have sexual intercourse with each other. In such cases it has been found that the boy was suffering from anxiety or did not have confidence in himself, and the girl had visions of being forced to marry or was afraid of the sex act itself. Boys and girls who do not have a regular partner sleep around wildly, throwing themselves indiscriminately at this person or that. Some girls notice that the boys are looking for them and play on this fact, going from one to the other, taking this one today and that one tomorrow. Constantly being without girls or without boys leads in the boy to the development of feelings of inferiority and in the girl to hysterical behavior. The boys begin to compare themselves with others who do have partners, and they imagine that they suffer from this or that defect. Those who pick up a girl here or there do not find any satisfaction because it is only their physical needs that are gratified. Therefore, they become emotional recluses and start to boast about their sexual experiences. Often they try too hard to find a girl; they roam around the streets, go to bars or dance halls, or visit depressing places of entertainment; and this ruins their lives. Others try to get a grip on their sexual problems by uselessly brooding over them, or they seek to master them through education. But what use is the best kind of enlightenment if they do not have partners or if, on the other hand, they do have partners but there is no opportunity to get together with them?

Let us summarize:

1. If young people are to have balanced, well-ordered sexual lives, they must be able to find partners. Let us stress once more that by "well-ordered" we do not mean eternally faithful, but satisfying.

2. Boys without girls become overly tense. Such young people are high-risk cases, because if they do not soon find a partner, their current dissatisfaction produces in them feelings of inferiority and the desire to boast. Also, if there is the slightest inclination to emotional illness, it leads to excessive indulgence in sexual fantasizing which, together with feelings of guilt associated with masturbation, can develop into serious sexual problems. For such young people, therefore, it is important as early as possible to take the necessary steps to clarify and solve the problem of finding partners. The longer the loneliness is permitted to last, ultimately manifesting itself in one way or another, the greater will be the need for a complicated course of treatment, although it is simply not feasible to provide such treatment for the majority of young people.

3. If such boys try to find a way out of their situation by running after girls in bars or dance halls, no one should believe that subjectively this is a solution. It is wrong to assume that the sexual phenomena that glitter like gold in these places are in fact the genuine article. Long years of experience have shown that the more sexual phenomena are thrust to the fore in a social group, the more disturbed, fragmented, and unsatisfying each individual's sexual life is, both internally and socially.

4. Young people suffer from severe sexual problems because their maturing sexuality conflicts sharply with prevailing conditions, not only as regards the education that they have received, but also as regards the social circumstances in which they find themselves.

WHAT THE SUPPRESSION OF YOUNG PEOPLE'S SEXUAL LIVES SIGNIFIES

What are the connections between the modern sexual order and the way in which it treats the sexuality of young people? What sense is there behind the sexual suppression of youth?

Most young people tolerate the suppression of their sexual lives by our society as something entirely normal and beyond reproach. Let us start by comparing the few young people who have satisfactory sexual lives with the others who are unable to free themselves from the morbid influences of morality and either live in abstinence, masturbate, or occasionally get involved in platonic love affairs and wallow in daydreams. We immediately notice that those who think more clearly on sexual matters openly rebel against school and church, while the sexually inhibited young people are usually "well behaved" and servile. This is not a chance phenomenon; there is a good reason for it. The suppression of sexual tensions and desires requires a great deal of energy in each person. This inhibits and impairs the development of activity, of intellect, and of initiative. On the other hand, if sexuality develops in a healthy and vigorous manner, people become more relaxed, more active, and more critical in their behavior.

Families and schools are nothing more than workshops for the production of weaklings and powerless creatures or slaves who have no self-confidence. The same attitude which a father requires of his children when they are young is often demanded of adults by greedy entrepreneurs and bureaucrats who understand nothing about our lives. An uncritical attitude, not "rocking the boat," no opinions of one's own—these are the characteristics that mark the relationship with the living vestiges of a bygone age. However, as an awareness of freedom develops within a family, so the attitude of the parents toward the children gradually changes; they experience life together as comrades and friends.

The difference between family slavery and family love, which is based on mutual respect and natural affinity, has not been understood. The slavery destroys us, and therefore we try to eliminate it. But the love of a father and a mother for their children and the love of the children for their parents is something that we must protect and preserve under all circumstances. We can do that only if we eradicate all kinds of slavery from these relationships.

The morality of abstinence is encouraged with particular strictness by both church and family during puberty, because it is precisely at this age that young people are starting to rebel against their enslavement. The sexual interests and strength of each individual revolt against it. In most families the period of puberty is when the sharpest conflicts occur between children and parents. Unless the young person's spirit has been completely crushed, he begins to revolt more and more against being forced to spend beautiful Sunday afternoons in the company of adults. All young people, whether girls or boys, sooner or later begin to understand more or less clearly that they belong somewhere else, among other people of their own age. They are bored with adults, and they desire air, sun, physical activity, and sexual relationships. If young people do not give some thought to these problems in time, then after a short and fruitless period of struggle against their parents, they sink into seclusion and become cut off from life.

Although the structured family is designed to render young people impotent and enslaved, sexual life and economic existence outside the protection of the family are often extremely dangerous for women and children, and the family and parental home play a very important role as protective institutions for them. Therefore, women are correct when they so often and so passionately defend marriage and family. They confuse the state in which they currently live with the possibilities of a rich life which may make this protection superfluous. Material independence is a quintessential part of emotional independence and of sexual health. Anyone who is economically dependent leaves himself wide open to all manner of enslavement.

But this struggle of youth against the backward views of the parental home should not prevent us from seeing the other side of the coin, namely, that these young people at the same time have deep ties to their parents and are emotionally as well as financially dependent on them. It is this dependence on parental care and authority which the Church immediately enters the fray to defend, equipped with all the machinery of stultification and platitudes about an avenging God, his eternal will, and his wise foresight, in its attempt to translocate marriage and family to divine regions far removed from the real world.

Let us take a close look at the area in which parental authority is most mistakenly applied, namely, wherever the sexual lives of their children are concerned. The means which such parental homes use to bring their children to heel consist essentially of sexually intimidating and crippling them and making them afraid of their sexual desires, thoughts, and deeds.

It is of little consequence to the outcome of this subjugation and suppression of young people whether the result is achieved through strictness or excessive tenderness. Both approaches bind the person equally firmly; usually both methods are combined, or one parent is brutal and the other excessively tender. The result is always that the young people lose their independence. When educators tell us that sexual freedom makes young people impossible to educate, we answer: Certainly, if the intention is to suppress them.

This sexual suppression of the children by their parents, to which is added the intellectual suppression by the school, the spiritual stultification by the Church, and finally the material suppression and exploitation by employer of employee, is the primary source of young people's emotional and sexual misery.

Since, however, the method used to create weakness of character consists of making young people afraid of sexual matters, the young people cannot recover their strength unless they are told firmly that their sexuality is something quite normal and natural, that it is right for them to stand up and fight for it, if necessary, against anyone who tries to suppress this aspect of their lives.

Before we come to the question of whether there are

ways and means nowadays to eliminate or simply alleviate the sexual distress of young people, we must discuss another point which so far has been too much neglected. While school often takes over from the parental home the task of emotionally suppressing young people, the Church is the main institution that continues the sexual suppression. We cannot emphasize often and forcibly enough that this suppression is the most important single factor contributing to the clouding of a person's emotions and the devastation of his inner life. It is no mere chance that, and indeed there is a very good reason why, the confirmation of young people in the Catholic Church coincides approximately with the onset of puberty. Children are under the influence of the Church up to the time of puberty, but when that time comes, the children, who are now adolescents, fall completely under the spell of the Church through the powerful instrument of the confession that is employed in the Catholic Church. It is an open secret that the central problem discussed during confession is not whether one has stolen anything, but whether one has committed a sin of the flesh, i.e., has the confessant masturbated or had extramarital intercourse. The confession serves to keep fresh in people's minds their feeling of sexual guilt, which was implanted in them as children by their parents in order to suppress their thirst for sexual knowledge and their sexual activities. During confession the young person is constantly told that sex is a terrible sin and that the highest authority, God, sees everything and punishes all the "crimes" that boys and girls commit in this connection. We will not discuss here the infinite misery that this message causes around the world in millions of young people approaching sexual maturity. This is the cause of their fears of masturbation, which crush their spirit and make them truly ill; this is the source of their anxiety states and severe hypochondriacal fears; finally, this is where the ground is prepared for later sexual disturbances.

If the study of youth were not in the service of hypocrisy, if human society were able to use its experience correctly and consistently to criticize conditions, then people would inevitably come to the same conclusion that we draw, namely, that the Church, because of its influence on the sexuality of youth, is an institution that exerts an extremely damaging effect on health. No punishment is too severe for people who, often in full knowledge of the damage that they are causing, not only get away with their indescribable misdeeds unpunished but are even very well paid for them.

These connections between the reaction of the Church and sexual suppression are not matters of little consequence. But we must also be able to prove to young people our assertion that the Church is reactionary. The Pope in his encyclical "On Christian Marriage"* called for Christian "morality" and marriage to be safeguarded. He wrote: "The code of love implies the superiority of men over women and children on the one hand and compliant subordination and willing obedience on the part of women (and children) on the other, as was described by the apostle in the following words: 'Wives (and children), submit yourselves to your husbands (and fathers) as to the Lord. For a husband has authority over his wife (and over his children) just as Christ has authority over the Church.'" Then, as an antidote to the distress suffered by young people, he recommended "religious exercises" and also warned the rich: "Those who live in excess should not use money and property for useless expenditures or throw

---

* Pope Pius XI, December 1930.—*Eds.*

218   WILHELM REICH

their wealth away, instead they must use that wealth for the support and benefit of those who are lacking even the most basic essentials."

If we were to tell young people that they are at odds with the Church because they are indulging in sexual activity, they would reply that with the aid of the Church and the Holy Ghost they are trying to find the strength to stop themselves from masturbating and to bring their sexuality under control. They should then be informed of the dangers to health and life that arise from subduing sexuality in this way. We must make them understand that physical strength and health as well as *joie de vivre* are much more important than phantasms about some afterlife. A blush of shame should rise to their cheeks when they are supposed to act in the same way and lead the same lives as old, dried-up men and women who have long left all their future behind them. To have grasped the fact that the Church is for the most part an institution that is supported and represented by old people means to become aware of one's own youthfulness and of one's youthful rights. We do not have to hurry to become senile at a young age.

The fundamental question is: Can hypocrites, moralists, and weaklings solve the problems of life for young people? Our reply is: No. For as long as the laws for living are written and imposed by weaklings, hypocrites, and impotent individuals, the mass of young people cannot hope to find a solution to their sexual problem, which is one of the most burning ones affecting them. In liberal circles there is much talk about the privations of youth, but we must take a close look to see how these people think, or claim to think, and how they actually behave. Are they really willing to accord young people complete sexual self-determination and a sexual life compatible with their age? Are they really prepared to acknowledge the need for

sexual intercourse among young people, where it is necessary and where its suppression causes health problems?
Are they willing to stop filling young people's minds with
dread of venereal disease by showing them dangerous educational films, during the screenings of which several young
people always faint? (In these films, 98 percent of the
emphasis is placed on filling the viewer with fear and
hammering home the ideology of abstinence, while only
2 percent of the emphasis is placed on the prevention of
venereal disease.) Are they willing to and can they officially
revoke the double sexual morality so that young men have
sexual relations with girls from their own social class and
not with prostitutes? Are they willing and does it fit in
with their whole way of thinking to distribute contraceptives unconditionally and free of charge to young people
in youth-counseling centers, which still need to be set up?
Will they terminate pregnancies in young people free of
charge at public clinics if contraceptive measures fail? Can
they solve the housing problem faced by young people so
that they no longer have to lead a caricature of a sex life
in doorways and cars, and so that each youth has the
opportunity to be alone with his partner? Are they, finally,
ready to educate children sexually in a way that enables
them later to take up a sexual life and to follow it correctly? No, because of its whole system of thought, weak-
hearted liberalism cannot solve the sexual problems of
young people. Liberals are quite incapable of coping with
any one of the burning issues of our age.

We do not wish to go into long theoretical discussions
here as to why the moralists can never change their sexual
system; this has already been explained elsewhere. If
sexuality frees itself from its old bonds, this is not because
the moralists help it to do so or want it that way, because,
in fact, it happens against their will. This is not only a

sign of the decay of this morality but also of all the old systems. The backward parental home and the Church have lost a great deal of influence among certain segments of youth. There is a lot of sexual fussing going on that looks like sexual liberation but in fact has nothing whatsoever to do with it.

What is the situation in reality? What is the mental and physical state of these young people as they indulge in this so-called more liberated sexual life? Surely the problems of young people have been made even *greater* by the fact that their sexual lives have been disrupted to such an extent in the parental home during early childhood and later on in school that they are usually inwardly unable to commence or lead any kind of satisfactory sex life. Has social welfare in the form of enlightenment, social aid, etc., increased at the same rate that morality has broken down? And is it not true that the sexual disturbances and sexually inspired suicides have increased enormously in recent years?

Clerics of every kind will say: "Yes, the sexual distress of adolescents stems from the fact that the morals of young people have grown lax." We would reply, and we can prove this statement right down to the last detail, that it was the sexual and economic suppression of youth that undermined this morality. The development of the world and the complication of human relationships guarantee that this morality will continue to break down and can never return. It is not we who have undermined this morality; nor did we create the moral crises; nor are we guilty of having destroyed the family. This has been brought about solely and wholly by the system of lies, dishonesty, and feebleness of spirit. We are merely fulfilling our task if we accelerate this painful process, which makes us all miserable, if we kill off the dying order in every respect and wherever we come across it so that we can create from it a new order of human relationships and finally do away with all manner of subservience, whether financial, emotional, or sexual. We live in a community of people not so that we can suppress and dominate each other or make each other miserable but so that we can better and more reliably satisfy all life's healthy needs.

Song of Youth

Stir up the smoldering fire of our will
Never weak tools of sad folly to be.
Plant deep in the flesh of all human beings
The seeds of natural dignity.

Away with all wars.
Put the mob to flight.
This world is our world and ours is the song;
Ours the just fight against all who suppress us;
Let happiness, love to us belong.

All you boys and girls—arise.
Fight the brave battle of your lives.

Stir up the smoldering fire of our will
Never weak tools of deception to be.
Tap the wellsprings of joyful existence.
Fertile life. WE BELONG TO THEE.

The works of Wilhelm Reich are published in cooperation with
The Wilhelm Reich Infant Trust Fund. Those seeking additional
information are advised to contact the trust fund at 382 Burns
Street, Forest Hills, N.Y. 11375, or The Wilhelm Reich Museum,
Orgonon, Rangeley, Maine 04970.